T0006174

——— The ———

BUSH CRAFT
ESSENTIALS
FIELD GUIDE

The
BUSH
CRAFT
ESSENTIALS
FIELD GUIDE

The Basics You Need to Pack, Know, and Do
━ TO SURVIVE ━
IN THE WILD

DAVE CANTERBURY
New York Times Bestselling Author of *Bushcraft 101*

ADAMS MEDIA
New York   London   Toronto   Sydney   New Delhi

Adams Media
An Imprint of Simon & Schuster, Inc.
100 Technology Center Drive
Stoughton, Massachusetts 02072

Copyright © 2022 by
Simon & Schuster, Inc.

First Adams Media trade paperback
edition October 2022

ADAMS MEDIA and colophon are
trademarks of Simon & Schuster.

For information about special
discounts for bulk purchases, please
contact Simon & Schuster Special
Sales at 1-866-506-1949 or
business@simonandschuster.com.

The Simon & Schuster Speakers
Bureau can bring authors to your live
event. For more information or to
book an event contact the Simon &
Schuster Speakers Bureau at 1-866-
248-3049 or visit our website at
www.simonspeakers.com.

Interior design by
Colleen Cunningham
Interior illustrations by Eric Andrews
and Claudia Wolf
Interior images © Clipart.com;
Getty Images/Timothy Messick;
123RF/Patrick Guenette

Manufactured in the United States of
America

1 2022

Library of Congress Cataloging-in-
Publication Data has been applied for.

ISBN 978-1-5072-1616-3
ISBN 978-1-5072-1617-0 (ebook)

Contains material adapted from
the following title published by
Adams Media, an Imprint of
Simon & Schuster, Inc.: *Bushcraft
Illustrated: A Visual Guide* by Dave
Canterbury, copyright © 2019, ISBN
978-1-5072-0902-8.

DEDICATION

*This book is dedicated to The Pathfinder School
instructors both past and present.*

*As the book lays out the basic system of teaching
from introductory through an intermediate level,
I cannot take sole credit for its development.
Some of these concepts have been a group effort and
are a shining example of what a group of like-minded
people can accomplish through cooperative effort.*

CONTENTS

CHAPTER 2. SELF-AID   43

CHAPTER 3. EMERGENCY SHELTER CONFIGURATIONS   59

CHAPTER 5. HYDRATION   91

CHAPTER 6. NAVIGATION AND SIGNALING   101

CHAPTER 8. LANDSCAPE RESOURCES (TREES)   137

⎯ Introduction ⎯

- *Self-Aid*
- *Shelter*
- *Fire*
- *Hydration*
- *Navigation and Signaling*

These are the five major wilderness survival priorities and the core of *The Bushcraft Essentials Field Guide*. Based on my experience surviving in nature, this essential information forms the basis of my 5 × 5 Survival System and will help you survive in the wild.

"Bushcraft" refers to the wilderness skills needed to survive and thrive in the natural world. To effectively practice bushcraft, you must learn and master the five major survival priorities. The purpose of my 5 × 5 Survival System is to provide a clear explanation of these major survival priorities without unnecessary information. The military uses the radio term "5 × 5" to describe a measure of signal strength and clarity—and it's that type of strong, clear communication that makes the 5 × 5 Survival System so effective.

This guide will first teach you about the five survival priorities and then will break down each priority into its five most critical points. In addition to the five priorities of short-term survival, *The Bushcraft Essentials Field Guide* will also cover the skills and information needed for long-term survival in the woods. From the importance of self-aid and the proper selection and construction of a campsite to securing water and fire for survival and navigating your way through the woods, this guide will highlight the critical elements of survival and how they come together in practice.

This is the survival system I use at The Pathfinder School, where I teach hundreds of students every year from all walks of life—civilians, law enforcement professionals, military personnel, search-and-rescue teams— how to survive in the wild. With this book, you, too, will learn how to practice the basics of outdoor survival.

—*Dave Canterbury*

— Chapter 1 —

SURVIVAL PRIORITIES

IN THIS CHAPTER YOU WILL BEGIN to learn about the five basic survival properties. You'll also learn about items you need to consider when making your carry kit, from knives and saws to ignition sources like ferrocerium rods. You'll also need some kind of cover, something that can help in repairs, some cordage, and other items in case you find yourself in an emergency situation. This chapter will show you all you'll need to be prepared.

5 SURVIVAL PRIORITIES

THE FIVE SURVIVAL PRIORITIES ARE self-aid, shelter, fire, hydration, and navigation and signaling. When in nature, you must constantly evaluate the order of these because they can change depending on the environment and situation. Understanding these priorities is key to the survival mentality that is crucial to the end goal of survival.

SELF-AID

The one survival priority that remains constant regardless of the scenario is self-aid. Self-aid must always be the number one priority because, without it, you may not be able to effectively accomplish the other four priorities. Keeping self-aid and safety at the forefront of your mind is essential to outdoor survival. You can learn more about self-aid in Chapter 2.

SHELTER

All survival scenarios revolve around core temperature control (CTC). If you get too cold, you will suffer the effects of hypothermia, and if you overheat, you will experience hyperthermia. Both of these conditions can be deadly, and many complications can arise from each one. Having the proper shelter is a major component of maintaining your core temperature and surviving. See more on shelters in Chapter 3.

FIRE

In addition to proper shelter, the ability to make and maintain a fire is imperative to CTC. Fire not only provides warmth; it also enables an abundance of survival necessities. Your ability to make fire allows you to disinfect water, cook and preserve food, regulate your body temperature, fire-harden tools, and signal for rescue in emergencies. Making a fire is not a difficult process, but if you don't have the proper materials or ignition methods, it can become extremely challenging. You'll learn more about making a fire in Chapter 4.

HYDRATION

Staying properly hydrated is vitally important for a variety of reasons, including to help metabolize food. Many people are unaware that water and caloric intake can affect both hypothermia and hyperthermia. Calories are burned to generate body heat, and, sooner or later, these calories must be replaced. To maintain CTC, you must make sure you stay properly hydrated. You need to be able to find and disinfect a water source to avoid the symptoms of dehydration, which can include dry mouth, headaches, and dark urine, and its consequences, like hypothermia and hyperthermia. You will learn more about hydration in Chapter 5.

NAVIGATION AND SIGNALING

If you were to become injured or lost during your outing, you may be able to rely on personal navigational skills to find your way out if the injury is not traumatic and if you planned for such an event before travel. This means packing first aid items for minor injuries and the proper navigation tools. It is also a good idea to tell someone where you are going in case you need to be found. If you have the proper navigation and signaling skills, you can increase your chance of being rescued and surviving. You can read more about navigation and signaling in Chapter 6.

> **BUSHCRAFT TIP**
>
> It is important to pack and carry tools to maintain CTC because it might be difficult or time consuming to find or create such tools in the wilderness, even if you possess the skills and resources. So, you want to pack items that are multifunctional (can accomplish more than one task) and that pertain to at least one of the five survival priorities. Some suggestions include multifunction kit items and a basic first aid kit (FAK), proper clothing for various conditions, an emergency sheltering system, several tools to start a fire in any weather, a groundwater disinfectant, a compass with a mirror, orange-colored materials, space blankets for signal panels, and orange bandannas or shemaghs.

5 Cs OF SURVIVABILITY

THIS SECTION LISTS THE CATEGORIES of items you should consider when building your survival carry kit. It is important to understand which criteria each item fulfills and how to use it effectively, as this can be the key to short-term survival and will aid in the longer term as well. For each of the following categories, consider packing a minimum of three items that will function individually and together. For an effective kit, be prepared to address major survival priorities first (and also multiple priorities with each item, if possible). This will help you make intelligent decisions based on your current skill level. When you build this basic carry kit, keep in mind that it should contain multiple items that address each priority.

CUTTING TOOLS

Cutting tools are used to craft various items and to process food. They are essential when practicing bushcraft. Because there are so many options, you must consider your specific needs and particular destination to select the right tools. Three essential cutting tools are a fixed-blade knife, a saw, and a Swiss Army knife or multi-tool.

KNIFE

The knife you choose is very important as a main tool, as it will most likely be attached to your body and will be your go-to for various types of work. It should always have a full tang, meaning it is made of one solid piece with scale materials attached to each side. You should look for a blade length between 4" and 5"; this makes the knife useful for processing materials up to 4" in diameter. A sharp spine on the blade is helpful so that it can be used like a spoke shave device for processing **tinder** materials or shaping wooden objects. Look for a high-carbon steel blade that can be used like a fire steel for the flint-and-steel ignition method of starting a fire. This type of blade can carve an emergency ignition source like a **bow drill** kit and can also throw sparks to ignite charred tinder sources.

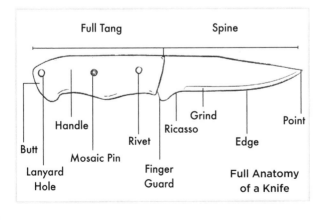

Full Tang   Spine

Handle   Grind   Point

Ricasso

Butt   Rivet   Edge

Mosaic Pin

Lanyard   Finger   Full Anatomy
Hole   Guard   of a Knife

SAW (FOLDING)

A saw for emergency use is in many ways much safer than swinging an axe or hatchet. Also, the lighter weight makes it easier to pack, and it will likely take up less space. The learning curve for safely using an axe compared to the easier-to-use saw can also be an issue. Selecting a saw is a matter of finding a trusted brand with a pruning-style folding blade. For general use, look for a minimum blade length of 8"–10". As with your knife choice, it's a good idea to find a blade with a sharp spine and a carbon blade, so it can function as another backup tool that will accomplish more than just crosscutting wood.

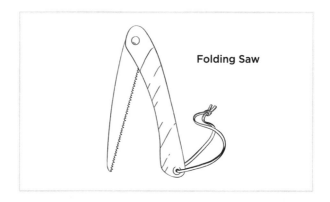

Folding Saw

SWISS ARMY KNIFE OR MULTI-TOOL

The choice between a Swiss Army knife (SAK) and a multi-tool (MT) is a personal one; however, the SAK has an advantage (depending on the model) because of its personal hygiene and first aid components. This may sound strange when speaking about a cutting tool, but remember that everything you carry should have multiple functions. A SAK will have a blade, possibly scissors (great for nail care), and generally an awl for making repairs, as well as other select tools. But many models also come with a pair of small tweezers and a toothpick, which, in my opinion, set this tool apart from the MT, as both are critical for care in the field.

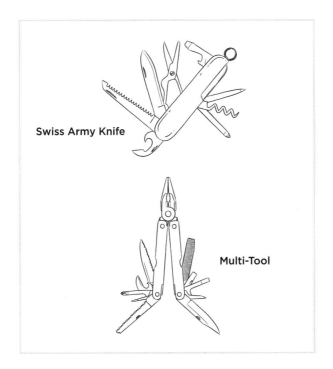

Swiss Army Knife

Multi-Tool

COMBUSTION DEVICE

Combustion devices are important elements of any kit. They are used to create fire, which not only helps preserve and cook food but also provides needed warmth. The three essential combustion devices are a Bic lighter, a **ferrocerium rod,** and a magnifying lens (which should be on your compass).

BIC LIGHTER

While the choice of lighters is a personal one, there are many reasons I prefer Bic lighters. I find that they can be easily rescued when wet and warmed when cold, and they have a heavy-duty construction that is difficult to damage. Use a screwdriver to remove the child-safety device to make it easier to rescue when wet and remember that even when the fluid has been used up, the sparking device will still ignite charred materials. Also remember that carrying several lighters in your kit, your pocket, and your pack won't take up much room or add much weight.

FERROCERIUM ROD

A ferrocerium rod for ignition is an important part of every emergency kit, but it should never be your first choice if open flame will do the trick. However, these rods have many long-term advantages: They are very dependable with dry tinder or charred materials, and large ones last a long time.

Some people don't realize that the makeup of these rods is not always the same, as some are harder and some are softer. A softer rod is a better choice for emergencies. The rod works by having some of its materials removed by an object that is sharper and harder than the rod itself. So, the softer the rod is, the easier it will be to remove the material. The larger the rod, the more material can be removed to create the hot sparks needed to ignite the material in a **tinder bundle**. Also, the larger the rod, the more contact time it has with the surface to remove material, and, again, the more hot sparks that will be able to reach the tinder.

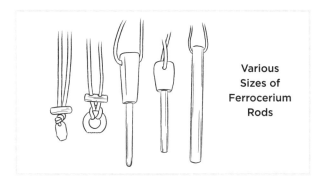

Various Sizes of Ferrocerium Rods

MAGNIFICATION LENS

Your compass should be equipped with some sort of **magnifying glass**. It should be powerful enough to ignite tinder that has been charred in full sun, giving you a renewable resource for ignition that cannot wear out and is long lasting. Many compasses come with a magnifying lens, but if yours doesn't, you should carry some kind of magnification lens in your pack.

Compass with Magnification Lens

BUSHCRAFT TIP

There are a few key things to remember about ignition and fire making. In an emergency, you want the easiest method of starting fire quickly, and most of the time, this will be open flame. Once that is taken care of, your next thought should always be to conserve expendable resources, like the fuel in a lighter. You should always have a "next-fire mentality." This involves making charred material with the first fire to ensure you can at least create a live ember for the next fires, which can be lit with any of the ignition sources you have on hand, including an empty lighter.

COVER ELEMENTS

Cover elements create a microclimate of protection and allow you to adapt to a given situation. Without proper cover elements, you put yourself at risk for exposure. The three essential cover elements are a reusable emergency space blanket, a 6-mil contractor bag, and an insulating blanket (either wool, synthetic, or down).

EMERGENCY SPACE BLANKET

You want to get a heavy-duty reusable space blanket for your kit; 5' × 7' size will work for an emergency. You don't want the Mylar-type blankets that are folded into small packages because these are difficult to reuse if you need to repack and move camp, and they are a bit flimsy to use in foul weather. Your emergency space blanket has many uses, but its two main functions are as an overhead **tarp** to protect you from the elements and as a blanket to convectively reflect heat from a fire to stay warm.

> **BUSHCRAFT TIP**
> Most emergency space blankets have at least a grommet hole in each corner. While this is not the most desirable method of attachment to a solid object for tie out, it can come in handy for emergency use.

6-MIL CONTRACTOR BAG

Plastic bags are measured in mils. One mil equals one-thousandth of an inch of thickness. You want a heavy-duty bag for your kit that can be used for anything from rain gear to a tarp to a mattress stuffed with debris. Lighter bags can handle these things, but a 6-mil bag can also act as a raised bed constructed like a stretcher to keep you off the ground.

INSULATING BLANKET

You will want to include a layer of insulation in your pack to trap body heat. This insulation can be different types of material, but some are better than others. A wool blanket, being fire-retardant, water-resistant, and insulative even when soaking wet, is the most effective and versatile option, but it will also be heavy to carry. Synthetic materials like Polarguard work well, and the Swagman Roll by Helikon is a great option for temperatures above 40°F (this can be made even more effective in colder weather by wearing a good base layer under your clothing). The advantage of this option is that it's lightweight and multifunctional as a blanket, a **sleeping bag**, a poncho liner, or a **hammock** under a quilt.

A 5' × 7' down blanket works great as insulation and takes up less room than the other choices. It would probably be as warm as wool depending on the down fill of the blanket, but it suffers dramatically when wet (as it loses its insulation properties) or around sparks from a fire because most down blankets are made from nylon (which can be flammable). But it is a great lightweight option if you can keep it protected from fire damage.

> When building a shelter kit, you obviously want the individual components to be multifunctional, but the key elements to consider are something to sleep on, something to sleep in, and something to sleep under.

CONTAINERS

Containers are simple but important components of any kit. Containers allow you to:

- Carry water over distances
- Protect your food sources
- Boil water for disinfection
- Use them as a cold or hot pack for self-aid
- Signal for rescue by using them as a sound chamber

The three essential containers are two water bottles and one cup.

METAL WATER BOTTLE

Metal containers for food and water are a must-have for survival kits because you can put them directly into a fire. In addition, if you don't have a filter of some kind to disinfect water, you can use a metal bottle to boil it. You can use it to cook food and make medicinal teas. You want a bottle with a wide mouth for easy filling and at least a 32-ounce capacity, as it may take up to four of these a day to keep you hydrated.

Metal Water Bottle and Nesting Cup

CUPS

The metal cup that nests under your bottle is an important element of your kit. It allows you to boil liquid or cook food and is another container to eat or drink from. It can also be a chamber for charring material when placed over the open mouth of the container and into a fire. It is smart to carry two of these cups even if you only have one bottle because you can put one on the top and one on the bottom of the bottle. Having something to drink from while making char or having two cups cooling while another bottle is boiling comes in handy.

CORDAGE

Being able to properly bind and lash materials is imperative to survival. Cordage allows you to bind and lash materials and to create other items. It is also helpful for trapping and fishing and a host of other tasks. It is important to consider the cordage you choose to carry with you. The three essential cordage suggestions are **parachute cord** (550), **bank line** (#36), and **tubular webbing** or mule tape.

PARACHUTE CORD

It's important to remember that most survival manuals of the twentieth century were largely copied from military text, and the military has a lot of parachute cord on hand, so soldiers are taught to use it. That does not necessarily mean this is the best type of cordage for you. I carry about 30' of parachute cord hanked up to use as a **ridgeline**. I always keep an end of the line loop at one end and stop knot at the other; also attached are two Prusik loops used to **toggle** a tarp or space blanket. This cordage can also be used for bipod-style shelters for a **lashing** and stakeout cord. Also, I generally have at least six shorter lengths of parachute cord of about 7' in the same hank configuration without the Prusik loops to use as utility cords in camp for anything from hanging a pack to a hasty tripod or even a temporary tourniquet if the need arises.

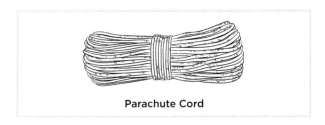

Parachute Cord

BANK LINE

Bank line is a lightweight and durable tarred nylon that is useful for fishing and net making, as it is easy to tie and holds knots well. It is a good survival cord because it is rot- and UV-resistant and will also remain dry. The line can be easily broken down into smaller fibers that remain strong, which allows you to use it in a number of ways that might require a thinner fiber, such as a fishing line or as thread for cloth repairs.

Bank Line

TUBULAR WEBBING

Tubular webbing is used for climbing because it has a very high tensile strength to prevent breakage. This is one of its advantages over rope, as well as the fact that it weighs less and takes up less room. When making improvised straps and such from this material, you'll find it much more comfortable over distances than rope. Because webbing is flat, you'll be able to carry more of it.

I recommend two 20' sections and one 50' section if room and weight allow. This material will do anything rope will do—and will do it a bit better in most cases, except for helping to start a fire. You can always carry some of each, as I do.

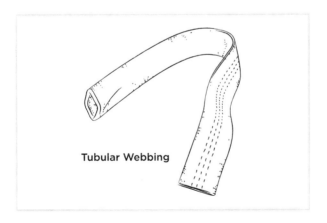

Tubular Webbing

5 Cs OF SUSTAINABILITY

THERE ARE FIVE MORE SIMPLE items that you can add to any emergency kit that will enhance whatever FAK you are carrying and will also enable the repair of gear and further signaling opportunities. Also, adding a base plate–style compass will aid in self-rescue if that is necessary. With these five items, you do not need to have three of each type.

COTTON MATERIAL

Bandanna, shemagh, spare T-shirt (orange is best)

One mainstay of my everyday kit is a 3' × 3' cotton shemagh. This is so multifunctional that a book could be written on this subject alone. A shemagh is a piece of material that can be adjusted and worn many ways to help protect your core temperature or as an additional piece of your kit, like a waist pack or belt. This makes a fantastic addition to any FAK, as it provides bandage materials as well as splinting ties and even an emergency tourniquet if necessary. For hygiene needs, it can be used as both a washcloth and a towel. You can create a coarse filter for water or evaporative cooling on a metal container in hot weather by wetting it and wrapping it around the container. Threads can be pulled from this fabric to sew on a loose button or patch a hole in your pants. If you are charring natural materials and there are no materials available from the landscape, these threads will create easy and quick char to help you with the next fire if you have used up all your emergency resources. Using orange-colored material is recommended because it can make a great waypoint marker for navigation or a signal panel or flag if the need arises.

CARGO TAPE

One roll of 2", one roll of 1" (always good to have a small roll outside the pack for easy access)

Cargo tape or duct tape provides a ready repair kit close at hand. It also has many uses as a first aid supplement and, due to the flammable adhesives, can be used as a flame extender in damp weather. Almost anything can be made from duct tape if you have enough of it. I always carry a 1" roll on the outside of my pack as a go-to for quick bandages on the trail as well as for immediate repairs.

COMPASS

*Needs to have a movable **bezel ring**, mirror, and mag-nification lens*

Your compass has several important features that go well beyond simple navigation. A mirror helps with

1
2
3
4
5
6
7
8
9

first aid, hygiene, and signaling. A magnifying glass can replace a lost or broken pair of reading glasses and help with first aid as well as fire starting. In addition to finding direction and subsequently helping you walk a straight line, the compass should have a sighting mirror that can be used for signaling or in self-aid to see a facial injury. If you have the right compass, it is a tool in itself that can accomplish many things. Judging height (this requires an inclinometer) and short distance across a dangerous area can be accomplished by the rule of right angles. It is a pocket measuring device that works with a printed map and can also be used to create maps with a real-time **PAUL (Positive Azimuth Uniform Layout)** method.

CANDLING DEVICE

This light should generally be a headlamp and not a flashlight. It can be used for signaling by either using its flash mode (if it has one) or moving your hand on and off the light to communicate SOS. If you have to perform self-aid at night, even if you are only changing a bandage, a headlamp will be an asset. Having a waterproof headlamp is important if it is used in foul weather. Another consideration is how the device is powered. Batteries can be replaced and spares carried, but there are models that charge by USB, or a simple charging brick (such as is used for a cell phone) can also recharge the light.

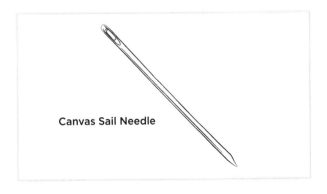

Candling Device

CANVAS SAIL NEEDLE

A canvas sail needle is a specific type of needle and not just any semi-large needle from a fabric store. A canvas sail needle is designed specifically for tent or sail **canvas**. This unassuming part of your kit can easily be taped to a knife **sheath** using duct tape and forgotten until needed. This tool can repair fabric or material, push holes through bark, and pop blisters or pick out splinters or other small debris from a laceration or abrasion.

Canvas Sail Needle

— Chapter 2 —

SELF-AID

S ELF-AID HAS TO BE YOUR first priority in an emergency. Obviously, if you are bleeding or injured in some incapacitating way, other tasks will be impossible or at least much more difficult unless you first address the injury. Not to mention that when it comes to bleeding, you may have limited time to stop the blood flow before you are completely incapacitated. This chapter does not discuss simple ailments like a sore throat or upset stomach, although some of these can be addressed once your main priorities are dealt with. Rather, this chapter covers immediate danger or injuries that stop you from working, which need to be your first concern.

Do not consider this as medical advice or a reason to forgo formal training in first aid. Also, do not construe this as a substitute for a first aid kit (FAK) of your choice. You only use the kit items you have as a supplement to materials either not available or in limited supply.

The following 5 Bs of Self-Aid section will discuss generally the kit items you should carry and how they pertain to self-aid issues. My book *Bushcraft First Aid* covers these topics in more depth. It is important to understand that all wounds should be cleaned and irrigated to remove debris and dirt. This can be done with an elevated water bottle, used as many times as necessary to clean the wound.

5 Bs OF SELF-AID

FIRST AID, WHEN APPLIED TO yourself, is known as "self-aid." This should be considered the cornerstone of your first aid training. When you are injured, it's crucial to remain calm and act rationally, because a momentary lapse in judgment could create a dangerous situation that you may not be able to address in a remote location without proper medical care. The 5 Bs of self-aid cover the main medical issues you might encounter in the wilderness. By knowing and preparing for these dangers, you can give yourself appropriate first aid treatment for common issues and emergencies.

BLEEDING

The way you deal with bleeding will depend on the type of bleeding you are experiencing. If blood is spraying or squirting from the wound in large amounts, you should immediately apply a tourniquet of some type. The general rule with non-arterial bleeding is direct pressure, elevation, tourniquet. Your first aid kit should have cotton material for bandages and duct tape to help secure them. In addition, a sturdy stick or even your folding saw can create a windlass for a tourniquet secured with duct tape.

You can use your cotton material to create pressure dressings to keep bleeding under control.

BREAKS, SPRAINS, STRAINS

Securing a possible break from movement and wrapping a sprain for support are key elements of self-aid. You should have cotton material and duct tape to deal with these types of injuries. Simple splints can be improvised with tool handles or local materials. Swelling can be controlled somewhat with a water bottle cooled in a nearby body of water and then held on the affected area. Elevating the injury will also help when possible. While not necessarily part of your main kit, you may be wearing a T-shirt or wicking layer made from a stretchy material that can be cut to create an impromptu bandage.

BURNS

Depending on their severity, burns can be a tricky thing. In third-degree burns, infection can set in very easily, so you should get medical help as soon as possible, especially if the burn covers a large surface area on the body. In general, keep burns damp and cool. You should have many tools in your kit that can accomplish this, such as a water bottle, cotton materials, and even plastic garbage bags to slow down evaporation on a bandage. Remember, however, that sealing a wound with plastic is like building an incubator for bacteria, so you will need to refresh these dressings often. One advantage to using kit materials (like gauze or cotton bandannas) to supplement bandages is that they can be cleaned with boiling water and replaced until you can get appropriate medical help.

BLISTERS

The best way to deal with blisters is to prevent them. Break in your boots before venturing on a long hike and make sure you have the right socks. If you get a hot spot, stop and cover it with duct tape to alleviate the friction. Powder your feet well and take frequent breaks to dry your feet out. If a blister does develop, cut a doughnut shape from your tape and cover it so the blister is centered in the hole. If you rip the roof off the blister and it becomes an open wound, then treat it as such and pad the area well before moving on. Remember that ashes from a campfire will work as an improvised foot powder, and you can collect these in the morning before leaving to use throughout the day if needed.

BITES AND STINGS

Obviously there are many types of bites and stings with just as many symptoms, so I will not try to address them all here. Some common symptoms like swelling can be treated with a cold water bottle. You

1
2
3
4
5
6
7
8
9

can remove stingers with a sterilized (by fire) canvas sail needle or the tweezers from your Swiss Army knife (SAK). Like other injuries, bite and sting symptoms can be very severe, and some can cause allergic reactions. There is no substitute for first aid training, and if you know you are allergic to certain venoms, be prepared and carry the appropriate medications.

SELF-AID

1

2

3

4

5

6

7

8

9

ESSENTIAL TIPS ON PERSONAL HYGIENE

PERSONAL HYGIENE IS JUST AS important as any other form of self-aid. Keeping yourself clean and your oral hygiene in check can save you from a potentially unpleasant situation.

HAIR AND SKIN

Using white ash from the fire is an acceptable substitute for soap, and you can use cotton materials to wash and dry yourself. These materials can then be cleaned for reuse. Ashes can also be used as a dry shampoo and as a powder for the underarms, groin, and feet. Washing clothing to remove dead skin cells and then smoking them over a fire to kill bacteria will keep you from getting prickly heat and will also control odor.

TEETH AND MOUTH

If you are not carrying a toothbrush, whatever you do, *do not* use a wooden twig to brush your teeth or remove something from your teeth and gums, as this is just asking for a splinter that will cause a lot more issues than a couple days of dirty teeth. You have a sail needle and possibly a plastic toothpick in your SAK, and you can scrub your teeth with a cotton

SELF-AID

1

2

3

4

5

6

7

8

9

material wrapped around a finger combined with charcoal or ashes for a toothpaste.

FEET AND NAILS

Keeping your feet clean and dry will also help to alleviate friction while hiking, so remember to remove your footwear and socks, clean them with a wet cotton material, and dust them with ashes to keep your feet in top shape. If your nails need to be trimmed, do it right away. Don't wait and hope they will be okay, because even the smallest nail can be an irritant over the miles and can cause an open wound. Use the scissors in your SAK (I recommend the Outrider model) for this job.

WASTE

Waste is an inevitable part of the outdoor experience and should be addressed in any text regarding hygiene. Cleaning up after you do your business should never involve the use of leaves or plant material unless you are very familiar with the type of plant, because it may irritate the skin or cause contact dermatitis. Cotton material can be used, cleaned, and reused.

NATURAL MEDICINES

BECOMING A KNOWLEDGEABLE HERBALIST CAN take years of dedication, research, and practical application. But when you're in the woods, you just need to know what you can do to make the pain go away or to relieve the swelling from a spider bite or to stop the bleeding from an errant knife slice. You will probably carry the solutions to some of these issues in your pack, but you can also find helpful materials in the landscape.

If you understand the natural resources around you, you can use many of them as temporary replacements for treatments that you may keep in your bathroom cabinet at home for things like a sore throat, headache, sore muscles, diarrhea, stomach upset, and gas.

In this section, we will concentrate on a single symptom or action we want to accomplish. If you have a stomachache, you can probably figure out why. You're hungry, you ate or drank something that didn't agree with you, or you have picked up a virus. So all you need to figure out is how to help relieve or counteract the symptoms. This is where knowing the plants in your local area comes into play.

The good news is that you don't need to know about many plants to take care of lots of issues.

Plants have two main components: primary metabolites and secondary metabolites. The primaries are what give the plant its growth—the carbohydrates and fibers that help make it a living organism. The secondary metabolites are what you want to understand in your quest for relief from a particular illness. These are the compounds that give the plant its taste, make it poisonous or not, give it color, and so on. They can also be minerals absorbed from the soil. These are the active components.

These secondary metabolites can have many different effects on the body both internally and externally, but by using the entire plant and not just a single metabolite or chemical constituent (like many modern pharmaceuticals), you can treat many different things. Simples are herbal preps that have only one main ingredient of plant matter.

Let's look at something to help you understand a bit more about herbal energetics (what plants do to your body). In herbal applications for this context, you are trying to treat one symptom with plant matter that has the opposite effect on tissue. The early Greeks called these influences the four bodily humors (wet, dry, cold, hot). If you have a hot condition, you want a cooling effect from the herb, and so on. Opposites create balance.

USE TASTE AS A GUIDE

The next thing you need to understand is taste. I will use simple terms for this discussion. Common tastes are astringent (drying/puckering), sour (cool), acrid (foul tasting), aromatic (spicy/warm), mucilaginous (wet, creates saliva), and bitter (leaves aftertaste). If you have properly identified the plant, you know if it is safe to place in your mouth. The taste can give you clues about how it will affect you both internally and externally.

Let's use astringent as an example. If I place a green plant leaf in my mouth, say, from a goldenrod, and it dries my mouth out, then I can deduce that it is astringent. It may also be slightly bitter or acrid, but the drying component is the key. If a plant is drying, then it can be used to treat wet conditions like bleeding, runny nose, and diarrhea. Some plants are used externally, and others are used internally, so it is important to understand how to use them.

COMMON PLANTS FOR HEALING

Do you need to know every plant in the woods to be effective at treating common ailments? No! You just need a short list of very common plants that will address the issues you may have to deal with. Remember, you are in the woods for a short time. You don't need to pass a kidney stone (hopefully) or cure a disease (hopefully)!

You are looking for simple treatments for those annoyances that make woods life less enjoyable, like upset stomach, headache, sore throat, constipation, toothache, cuts and abrasions, and burns.

PLANTAIN

Plantain grows close to the ground, and its most distinguishing characteristics for identification are the large veins on the back of the leaf—and also the spike that rises when the plant goes to seed. Plantain treats infection or venoms from under the skin (as with an insect sting), or a festered splinter. A plantain salve can also help with minor burns and abrasions.

Plantain Leaf

DANDELION

Dandelion is bitter, which means it activates your digestive system, and can be used as a diuretic. A dried mint and dandelion infusion is good for upset stomachs and can help relieve diarrhea. Dandelion also makes a good coffee substitute.

Dandelion

SWAMP VIOLET

Swamp violet blooms from the end of February to the end of April. It can alleviate symptoms of dry tissues, such as a dry sore throat or cough. It also aids in regulating the digestive system, such as bloating, gas, and constipation, as it is a mild laxative.

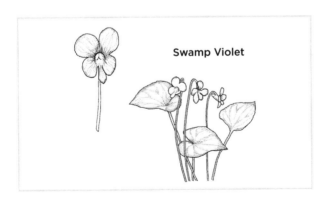

Swamp Violet

BONESET

Boneset can help cold-tissue states, such as cold, flu, mild hypothermia, and constipation. It's a warming stimulant and, when taken in excess, can be a laxative. The distinguishing feature of this plant is the stem that appears to grow through a single opposing lance-shaped leaf.

Boneset

JEWELWEED

Jewelweed contains a compound called lawsone in its leaves, which has been proven to have antihistamine and anti-inflammatory properties when used as a salve (external use only). It grows in large patches, and its flowers are orange when blooming.

Jewelweed

PREPARING HERBS

When you are in the woods, you want to find the simplest way to use the plants you need. You are only carrying what you need, so you should be able to prepare and use herbal remedies easily. Here are some common preparation methods.

- **Just eat it!** If you don't have time for prep and need to use the plant internally, just consume it. You should have already determined it is safe. Eating too much in most cases will not harm you. If you can't stand to eat too much due to the taste, you probably don't need that much anyway. Your body knows. It is not like pills, where two are good and five will kill you.
- **Spit poultices.** The plant is chewed, mixed with saliva, and held on the wound with a dressing.
- **Infusion.** Prepare an infusion like a tea. Pour hot water over the herb and cover it to steep for 10–15 minutes.
- **Decoction.** A **decoction** is made up of roots or barks that are boiled in water and strained. Boiling for 10–20 minutes will suffice if the stock is processed down. Both infusions and decoctions can be gargled or consumed.
- **Fomentation.** Fomentation is done by soaking a rag in hot liquid from an infusion or decoction and applying it to the skin.

- **Wash.** Similar to a fomentation, a wash is used to rinse an area or flush a wound site.

> If you're suffering from an itch because you got too close to a bunch of poison ivy, any plant or tree with a high concentration of **tannins** will constrict your pores and will help push the oils to the surface where they can be neutralized more easily or scrubbed off. Oaks, both red and white, have high concentrations of tannins even in the leaves. You can create a cold infusion or a tea that will help as a wash. Do not use warm liquid on an itch, however, as this will only aggravate the condition.

BUSHCRAFT TIP

— Chapter 3 —

EMERGENCY SHELTER CONFIGURATIONS

BUILDING A SHELTER TO EITHER protect yourself from weather or to conserve existing body heat is a critical skill for survival and one of the top priorities to address if an emergency occurs. You should have materials in your kit that will help you build shelters so you have something to sleep on, something to sleep in, and something to sleep under. A proper shelter will help you battle heat-loss/stop-loss mechanisms (more on this in this chapter) especially when combined with fire. This chapter also discusses site selection, as configuration is based on several factors like available resource anchor points, surrounding terrain, and the use/availability of fire.

1

2

3

4

5

6

7

8

9

5 Ws OF CAMPSITE SELECTION

ONE OF THE MOST IMPORTANT decisions you can make is where you set up camp. You need to carefully consider any area you choose as a base camp for an extended period because of the eventual depletion of nearby resources. The 5 Ws are a simple yet important checklist of concerns to consider when choosing a proper camp location.

WOOD

When you are considering a camp location, you should plan how easy it will be to maintain a fire during the time you are there and whether there are materials nearby for a signal fire if needed. Check if there are enough natural resources around you by gathering materials from several yards away from camp and then work your way in to ensure you have enough for a few days if needed. Is there deadwood at ground level so you do not need to chop or cut anything? How about tinder sources like dry inner barks for fire starting? Wood is an even bigger consideration in colder weather because you will need much more to maintain body warmth during a possible freezing night.

WATER

Water is a major concern if you plan to be in a camp for more than a few hours. You will need a source fairly close by to collect from. You should be selective about the water source; for example, a running stream is better than a standing pool, and water that is clear and does not require a lot of filtering to remove turbidity will be easier to manage in an emergency. The water's quality may be difficult to judge by looks alone, but discolored and stained water should be avoided if possible.

WEATHER

There are many types of weather—rain, snow, wind, heat—that you should consider when selecting a site and **pitching a tarp**. Prevailing winds can be used as a gauge if there are no obvious weather conditions when you are setting up camp. You should be attentive to impending weather as well as current weather. Winds that blow rain into your shelter can make for miserable nights, but you may want a crosswind to help feed a fire through the night in cold weather.

WIDOWMAKERS

A dead standing tree (referred to as a **"widow-maker"**) can be an issue at any time, not just when the winds are high. Large dead branches hanging in tree canopies can dislodge and cause injury or death.

You will want to ensure that your camp is well away from these hazards and understand exactly how far a tree can fall if it comes down. Also, look at living trees that are normally brittle in extreme weather; for example, aspens and poplars can sometimes snap off in high winds, so be aware of these dangers as well.

WILDLIFE

Wildlife is anything that walks, crawls, or slithers, whether on four legs, no legs, or six to eight legs. Anything from insects to mammals can cause issues. Never camp on a game trail, and always clear the area around camp to keep crawling insects at a distance. Check for nearby nests on the ground and in the trees for bees, wasps, and hornets. Food attracts some wildlife, so if you have food on hand, you may need to suspend it from a tree branch to keep it away from wildlife. Make sure you process any food you find well away from your camp.

5 SHELTER NECESSITIES

THERE'S A LOT TO CONSIDER when deciding on and building your shelter. The following five necessities outline the main things to consider when it comes to constructing your shelter and deciding where you'll sleep. As discussed, regulating your core body temperature is imperative to survival. It is essential to keep that in the front of your mind, because you need to factor heat loss prevention into where you decide to sleep.

UNDER

Having something to sleep under is critical for repelling rain, snow, and wind. Depending on the configuration of your shelter, you should be able to manage most weather conditions with a basic tarp.

> **BUSHCRAFT TIP**
>
> It is worth noting that an emergency tarp can be used with the reflective side down to take advantage of convective heat exchange or with the reflective side up to create shade and reflect solar radiant heat away.

ON

You will need something to sleep on top of to help battle heat conduction from the ground in cold weather. If you're using natural materials, like in a **browse bag**, you'll need 4" of compressed material.

INSIDE OF

Creating some kind of structure that you can sleep inside of to trap dead air space will help battle convection and trap radiant body heat in cold weather.

INSULATION

Insulation starts with clothing. In cold weather, a good merino wool base is essential, and there is nothing wrong with sleeping fully clothed. You should, however, avoid sleeping in boots or shoes because your circulation could be restricted, which will make your feet colder. Also, if the shoes or boots are waterproof, your feet will sweat all night, becoming colder as the night goes on.

BREATHABILITY

Breathability is an important aspect when considering clothing or a bag/**bivy bag**. Breathable materials allow moisture to escape so you do not wake up wet. Wool is a breathable material and is a good option for clothing as well as layering and blankets if weight is not a concern. For emergencies, you may want something lighter in weight like Polarguard insulation.

5 EMERGENCY SHELTER CONFIGURATIONS

WHEN IT COMES TO PUTTING together your shelter, there are multiple options to choose from. You will need to consider a variety of factors before selecting the appropriate configuration for your situation, including weather, landscape, available materials, and how long you plan on staying. These five shelter configurations are easy to put together relatively quickly.

FLY

A fly configuration means that none of the tarp is on the ground (hence **flying a tarp**). The tarp is either laid across the ridgeline or connected at two points; all other points are tied down by guylines and these are connected at anchor points.

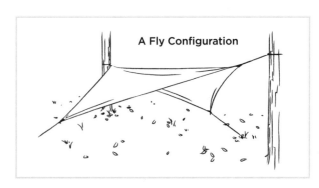

A Fly Configuration

A-FRAME

An **A-frame shelter** is typically made by lashing a simple cross pole between trees, adding several more saplings at a 45-degree angle to the ground on one side, then weaving in horizontal vines or cuttings (see the following image). However, you can make the same shape with a tarp. In that version, the tarp is draped over or connected at two center points to the ridgeline, with the four corners staked to the ground. A modified A-frame is made with the tarp, or natural materials if a tarp is unavailable, on a **diamond layout** across the ridge and the two opposing corners staked.

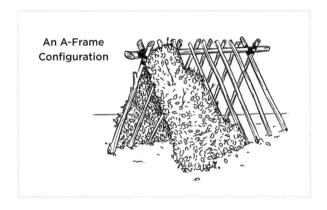

An A-Frame Configuration

LEAN-TOS

Lean-tos are used with two outside points connected to the ridgeline and the other two staked to the ground with the tarp on an angle. The height of the ridge will dictate how much heat is held in the tarp.

A Lean-To Shelter Made of Natural Materials

WEDGE

Wedge setups, also known as plow points, use a single anchor point on a ridgeline, a bipod, or a stationary object like a tree. Using a diamond layout of the tarp, the other three points are staked to the ground. Again, the height of the ridge will dictate how much heat will be kept or released. This setup provides a greater area of coverage but still allows room for a small fire for warmth outside the front.

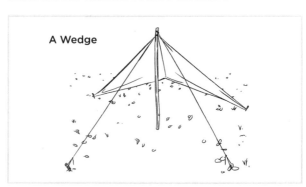

A Wedge

RAISED BED

For a raised bed, you will need to cut some material and use two 6-mil bags from your kit. By making two large tripods and cutting the bottom from the bags, you can slide horizontal poles into the bags and use the tripods on opposite ends to support the cot-style bed. You can then use the space blanket as a tarp on a ridgeline. The other advantage to this setup, besides getting you off the ground, is the ease of stuffing the bags with debris for insulation.

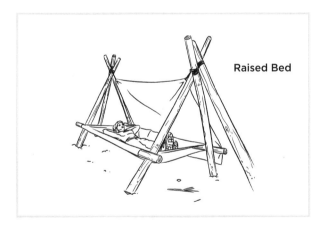

Raised Bed

BUSHCRAFT TIP

An easy way to remember the difference between these configurations is that there are zero corners of the tarp touching the ground on a fly, two corners touching the ground on a lean-to, three corners touching the ground on a wedge, and four corners touching the ground on an A-frame.

5 COMPONENTS OF AN EMERGENCY SHELTERING KIT

Since you may not always know when you will need to set up a shelter—for example, if a weather emergency requires you to set up camp unexpectedly—it's important to keep the following materials together in a sheltering kit. With these components, you will be able to construct an emergency shelter to provide coverage and protection from the elements.

QUICK DEPLOYMENT RIDGELINE AND EIGHT UTILITY ROPES

This kit should consist of a 30' piece of 550 parachute cord with a 2" bowline on one end (an overhand knot loop will work) and a stop knot on the other end. Attached to this should be two Prusik loops about 6" in diameter (used to attach tarp corners with toggles and adjust for tightness). For easy access, this line should be stored with six stakes of your choice. The eight utility ropes are miniature versions of the ridgeline (without the Prusik loops); these are used for guy lines or extensions of the ridge through loop-to-loop or toggle-to-loop connections.

SIX STAKES

It is much easier to just carry stakes than to rely on materials being available at your site. It also takes time to fabricate good stakes, and you may have to put up your shelter quickly. Your choice of stakes will be dictated by terrain, environment, season, and weight.

TWO 55-GALLON CONTRACTOR BAGS

These bags should be a minimum of 3 mil, but 6 mil will be much more durable. They have many uses in an emergency, but for sheltering, they can be made into a dry ground barrier and/or a mattress when stuffed with debris and closed with duct tape. If you're going to make a raised bed, you should use a 6 mil. Remember that 4" of compressed material is the rule to battle heat loss. The bags can also be used as an emergency rain poncho or tarp extension, as well as a backpack cover or to keep firewood dry.

ONE EMERGENCY REUSABLE SPACE BLANKET (5' × 7')

When it comes to space blankets, you don't want the ones that are thin and folded very small, as they are not durable even in the short term, and if you need to move camp or change shelter configurations, that can be troublesome at best. A 5' × 7' blanket will not add a lot of weight, but it will give you enough

1

2

3

4

5

6

7

8

9

coverage for the short term, unless you are exceptionally tall.

ONE INSULATION LAYER

The type of insulation you choose will depend on the weather conditions and how much weight you want to carry. There are many different kinds on the market, including wool blankets, poncho liners, Swagman Rolls, and ultralight sleeping bags. Remember, this is an emergency kit item, so don't think about packing things you will already have if you planned to camp. For a kit you take on a day hike, you will still want an insulation layer, like a survival bivy bag or even a lightweight poncho liner (this is a good multifunctional item especially if you carry a poncho anyway). Snugpak's insulating Jungle Blanket is a good lightweight option. Your clothing makes up for some insulation if you have dressed properly and packed accordingly for any weather changes.

CRITICAL FUNCTIONS: HEAT-LOSS/STOP-LOSS MECHANISMS (THERMOREGULATION)

As DISCUSSED PREVIOUSLY, THE KEY to survival is core temperature control (CTC). You will suffer the effects of hypothermia if you get too cold, and if you overheat, you will suffer from hyperthermia. It is important to be aware of the ways in which your body thermoregulates. The proper shelter protects against the factors that may cause heat loss and therefore throw off your thermoregulation.

CONDUCTION

Conduction is the loss of heat through contact with a cold object like the ground. To maintain proper CTC, you need to avoid conduction while you sleep. Bedrolls, blankets, and insulation layers help combat heat loss and keep your body temperature regulated.

CONVECTION

The basis of convection is that warm air rises and cold air sinks. Therefore, when heat from a low fire is reflected toward the body as it cools, it will rise and the warm air will replace it, causing a type of rolling current called convection. This can be taken advantage of by setting up a campfire backing the height of the shelter's ridge and an opposing space blanket shelter to reflect the heat and create convection within the shelter.

RADIATION

Radiant heat comes from sources like the sun or a fire. With fire, you need to be aware of the rule of inverse squares. In simple terms, whatever heat you feel from a radiant source like a fire will be reduced as you move farther away. So, if you are, say, 3' from a fire, you will feel 100 percent of the heat at that distance. If you move 3' farther away, you will only get 25 percent of the same level of warmth.

PERSPIRATION

When you sweat, several things are happening. First, you are dehydrating, but your body is trying to take advantage of evaporative cooling by opening the pores and wetting the skin. If that moisture is trapped in layers of clothing, the water cannot evaporate, and it makes the clothing wet, in which case you will have a problem in cold weather. In arid environments, if you take in plenty of fluids, you can take advantage of this process to cool down.

RESPIRATION

We all inhale cold air in winter and exhale hot air from our core; this exchange can also eventually cool our core. Breathing through the nose can help warm the air before it reaches the core, and using your cotton material as a balaclava will also aid in retaining moisture and warmth in winter.

— Chapter 4 —

FIRECRAFT

FIRE IS THE RESOURCE THAT many consider second only in importance to a good cutting tool. Fire is critical for preventing cold-weather injury and providing general comfort around camp in cold environments. Fire can be used to disinfect water, cook and preserve food, prepare medicines, and keep bugs at bay. Building a fire in an emergency is imperative to your overall survival.

5 ELEMENTS OF FIRE

To BUILD AND MAINTAIN A healthy fire, it is important to understand the elements that contribute to it. Heat, fuel, oxygen, combustibility, and surface area all contribute to a successful build. Careful consideration and construction help to keep fires burning. The importance of a strong fire cannot be emphasized enough, and by understanding the elements of fire building, you will avoid wasting materials and time if the fire goes out.

HEAT

You must provide heat of some sort to effectively create fire. This is the first of the three legs in the triangle of fire building; the other two are fuel and oxygen (which will be discussed in the upcoming sections). Without this heat, ignition will not take place. A highly flammable material like a charred cloth must reach approximately 800°F to combust. Open flame is much hotter than this, as are the sparks from a ferrocerium rod. Even the sun magnified through a magnifying glass with a 5x magnification level will become much hotter than 800 degrees in a very short time. More primitive methods of fire making like the flint-and-steel method (removing minute materials from carbon steel with a stone) create sparks that meet the 800 degrees threshold, but because their temperatures are so low, it takes a very combustible material like char to effect ignition. The better the device you have and the hotter it is, the more marginal the tinder source you can use for fire lighting.

FUEL

Fuel is what the fire feeds on and consumes. In the beginning stages, this fuel should be small and soft. The fuel you begin with becomes your tinder bundle or **bird's nest**, but as the fire grows, it will need a longer-lasting fuel source like **kindling**. Eventually, the fire will need what is considered a longer-term fuel of large sticks or logs, split or whole, depending on what is available and on the fire's size. The fuel used for starting a fire depends on factors like weather, humidity, available kindling materials, and so on. Some fuels have accelerant value from the volatile oils within the wood, like **fatwood** from pine and birch bark. These types of fuels are preferable in wet conditions and add longevity in the initial heat source to damp kindling materials. Most of the time, inner barks are preferable for tinder bundles and bird's nests, as opposed to materials like grasses, as barks have more longevity to provide open flame after ignition to damp materials.

OXYGEN

Airflow is critical to fire, and it is this leg in the triangle of fire building that we restrict to effectively char the material. Maintaining a flow of air to the base of the fire will create an updraft, known as the **Venturi effect**. Leaving material loose and messy is always better than a **fire lay**, which is organized and tightly constricted and thus leaves fewer gaps for flames to climb. Remember that heat rises, and airflow from the base will accelerate this action. Controlling the three legs of your fire and manipulating them to the current conditions and materials are the keys to a successful fire.

COMBUSTIBILITY

In simple terms, combustibility means how easily a material will ignite. The denser the material, the harder it is to burn. The larger the material initially, the harder it is to initially ignite. This is why we speak of the three key elements of a fire lay as being tinder, kindling, and fuel. It is a progression of materials that are easy to ignite and faster burning to those harder to ignite, but that burn much longer once ignited. You will always want highly combustible materials for getting the initial fire going, and then longer-lasting and harder materials that are less combustible for longer-term fuels.

I recommend planning for your next fire immediately after starting your first one. In an emergency, you might need to use most of your available fire resources, compromising your expendable materials in the process. Once you have created your first fire and dealt with your emergency—for example, warming needs or disinfecting water—start planning your next fire. You never know what might happen in the next few hours: Fires can go out overnight and burn to ash, or rain can render a fire useless for relighting from coals. By charring your materials, you can help ensure that you will at least have a live ember to work with, and you can then begin to conserve the resources you have left. Charring is accomplished by placing a natural material like cotton or punky deadwood (soft, rotten wood usually found in the center of a tree or log) into a container like a stainless steel water bottle, covering it with a cup to create a chamber that restricts oxygen from entering, and then placing it into a fire. This will superheat the materials inside and carbonize them, creating char. The specific quality that makes char desirable is that any small hot spark will ignite it and create a nice hot ember, even if your tinder is a bit damp. In addition, you now have a material you can combust with every fire-starting method you are carrying. This allows you to conserve resources from your kit and use, for example, open flame only when needed for another emergency like lighting a signal fire quickly.

SURFACE AREA

The surface area is the sum of all the areas of all the shapes that cover the surface of the object. When looking for fire-starting materials, try to find materials that can be broken down to increase the surface area. For example, inner barks can be worked down to almost hairlike fibers, and a large bundle of these gives plenty of surface area not only for sparks to land but also for small fibers to combust quickly in contact with flame. Outer barks like birch that contain volatile oils will work the same way, and fine, thin shavings of materials like fatwood will work much better than just a sliver of wood.

FIRECRAFT

1

2

3

4

5

6

7

8

9

5 IGNITION SOURCES

THE FOLLOWING FIVE TYPES OF ignition cover the basic ways a fire can be started. From primitive methods like friction to the use of objects with chemical or electrical combustion, it's important to be prepared to start fire in a number of ways, and you carry in your pack the tools you need to start a fire.

FRICTION

In my opinion, using tools like the bow drill and hand drill to create friction fires are last-resort methods, although one can be very adept at their application. Unless a proven set is carried, these tools can be tricky to use reliably because of variables like material availability, moisture, energy level, and so on. With that being said, you should strive to learn these skills at an intermediate level, as many lessons in material selection, manipulation, and variability reduction within the process can be learned and applied to other things.

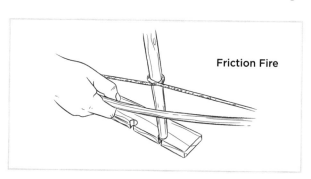

Friction Fire

PERCUSSION

Percussion ignition is performed by striking objects in glancing blows, such as iron material and a harder stone like flint, quartz, or chert. The flint-and-steel method is very reliable if you are employing a next-fire mentality, as this method requires charred materials. If you are lucky enough to be camping in northern areas where true tinder fungus (*Fomes fomentarius*) or another material that will ignite with a low-temperature spark grows naturally, you don't need to rely on charred material. But even this material is susceptible to weather and the specimen's condition. The best material will almost always be something charred. Again, this is an intermediate skill in many ways, but with a next-fire mentality and cotton material in your pack, you should have a basic understanding of it.

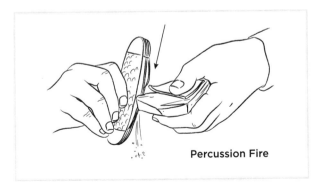

Percussion Fire

SOLAR

Ignition by sunlight is a basic skill everyone should practice if only for this method's renewability and longevity. Many natural sources can be ignited by the sun using a magnifying glass and any charred materials. One of my favorite methods is to take a tightly woven ball of processed bark from a poplar or cedar and create a small coal within the ball using the sun's heat, then transfer it to a bird's nest for ignition. If there is aspen punky wood in the area, it will also create a burning ember if it is first charred. This method relies heavily on planning or finding particular resources.

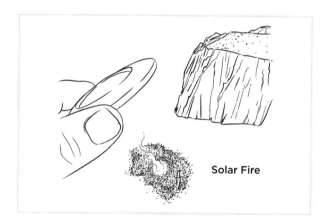

Solar Fire

CHEMICAL

Although even wood fires could be considered a chemical-reaction fire, we will discuss only liquid chemicals in this section. Chemical-reaction fires are not recommended, as the chemicals that were once used (and were at one point multifunctional for self-aid) are no longer considered the best application or treatment, so they have fallen out of fashion. With that being said, any two chemicals that create intense heat when mixed would be considered a chemical-reaction fire. Old-school fire starting was accomplished by mixing potassium permanganate with glycerin if one carried this in their first aid kit (FAK).

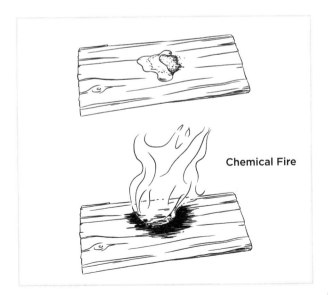

Chemical Fire

ELECTRICAL

Shorting any hot circuit will cause heat at the source of the short. In simple terms, this means connecting the positive and negative terminals of some sort of battery. It will take at least 3 volts or two AA or AAA batteries to create enough spark to ignite something like thin wires of steel wool. The higher the voltage, the easier this will be. However, as with some of the other methods, you don't want to carry something like steel wool just for this, and you don't generally need large-voltage batteries for a normal headlamp. I consider this to be an intermediate-level skill but largely unnecessary except for the advantage of having this as part of your knowledge base. For the sake of argument, if you were stranded with a vehicle battery and jumper cables, you would have an easy fire-starting source with minimal effort, and if you have a bit of gas, well…bonfire, I suppose.

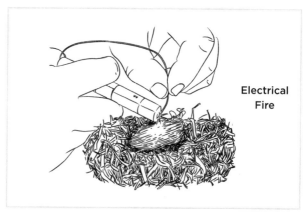

Electrical
Fire

5 USES FOR FIRE

FIRE IS ONE OF THE most useful tools you have in a survival scenario and even in a typical camp setting. Following are some uses for fire.

CTC (CORE TEMPERATURE CONTROL)

Regulating your core temperature control (CTC) is one of the most important things fire can do in an emergency, and even if creating a shelter is not immediately feasible, fire can keep you from freezing as long as you have material available. Much of what was discussed in Chapter 3 also plays a part in CTC, but this is one of the main functions of a fire in camp.

WATER DISINFECTION

Making groundwater potable and removing contaminants is very important. Boiling water will remove most of the pathogens but not chemicals or heavy metals. At normal altitudes below 5,000', once the water comes to a rolling boil, that is enough contact time under heat to kill all live waterborne threats.

COOKING

One of the oldest uses for fire is cooking and preserving food sources. From heating up canned goods to cooking game that you have trapped and hunted,

1
2
3
4
5
6
7
8
9

fire is imperative to providing sustenance. When you're cooking any type of meat, boiling will retain the most nutritional value. In addition to the meat, you can drink the broth, as it contains essential fats. And remember, fires are for warmth and coal beds are for cooking. Always let fires burn down to develop a large coal bed for cooking needs.

CHARRING MATERIALS

With a next-fire mentality, you have to think about charring materials as a means of creating a live ember to make the next fire easier. Char is a simple form of superheating natural materials and not allowing oxygen to create combustion. Once cooled, this material will ignite with a low-temperature spark like true flint and steel, a simple flick of sparks from a ferrocerium rod, or even a lighter that has run out of fluid.

SIGNALING

Signal fires are one of the best ways to attract attention from the ground to the air in an emergency. Lighting a signal fire is the same as building any other fire—just think bigger. The main thing to remember is that you must create an updraft to raise the smoke plume, so oxygen at the base is imperative. Take all the usual precautions when building and tending the fire. An out-of-control signal fire can do a lot of damage and endanger your life.

— Chapter 5 —

HYDRATION

ONE OF THE FIVE MAJOR survival priorities, hydration is key to keeping your body functioning in a healthy state. You would not be able to hike, build your campsite, or hunt and gather food if you were not properly hydrated. Unfortunately, staying hydrated is not as simple as just finding a source of water. That lake, stream, or other body of water contains contaminants that are harmful to ingest. To survive in the wilderness, you must know how to treat your water source so that it is safe to drink. Using the available methods to stay properly hydrated while in the woods requires knowledge and planning. You need the proper tools and equipment to process and clean the water you find. This chapter will provide you with the essential knowledge to stay hydrated and healthy in the wilderness.

5 WATER CONTAMINANTS

THERE ARE FIVE MAIN TYPES of contaminants in water that can render it unsafe for consumption. Removing them or rendering them inert might require multiple methods. Some contaminants cannot be immediately addressed without a certain type of filter, and even that may not be 100 percent effective. You must be very selective about the water source you choose (if you have a choice). In this chapter, you will learn how to disinfect water using materials from your kit: prefiltering and then boiling the water.

Now, this method may not address all the issues, which is why careful selection of the water source is so important. According to the WHO (World Health Organization), "Nearly 25 percent of the global population (1.8 billion people in 2012) is consuming fecally-contaminated water. This water can contain bacteria, protozoa, and viruses that can cause a variety of diseases in humans, most notably gastroenteritis."

TURBIDITY

Turbid water is hard on any filter system you may be carrying, but most folks don't like drinking debris in their water. The debris also gives pathogens something to latch on to, so turbid water needs to be filtered if possible. You can use the cotton material in your pack as a coarse filter by placing it over the mouth of a bottle at the collection source. A Millbank filtration bag (like the Brown Bag by Rupert Brown) will remove turbidity but will not make the water potable, so you will still need to disinfect the water.

CHEMICAL (INDUSTRIAL/AGRICULTURAL)

Chemicals from industrial waste, agricultural pesticides, heavy metals, and so on cannot be removed with a simple filter-and-boil method. There are some filters on the market, like the Grayl, that can remove some of these materials, but unless you have a high-grade filter that can effectively remove chemical waste, you should not drink this water.

BACTERIAL (HUMAN/ANIMAL)

Bacteria from waste are one of the main concerns you must consider when collecting a groundwater resource in remote areas. Filtering and boiling will remove bacteria, but you should understand contact times when boiling water. At elevations below 5,000', a good rolling boil should be enough to render bacteria inert; above this elevation, you need to boil water longer because water boils at a lower temperature at these higher elevations. A good rule is maintaining a rolling boil for 2–3 minutes before consumption.

PROTOZOA (CRYPTO/GIARDIA)

Like most things that can make you sick from drinking groundwater, you cannot see protozoan bodies with the naked eye, so it is important to filter and boil using the same protocol as listed for bacteria.

VIRUSES

Water-transmitted viral pathogens are considered moderate to high health risks by the WHO and can lead to conditions like rotavirus, hepatitis, and norovirus. Most of these viruses are associated with gastroenteritis, which can cause diarrhea, abdominal cramping, vomiting, and fever—but some viruses can have much more serious effects. Boiling water will help eliminate water-transmitted viral pathogens.

5 BASIC DISINFECTION METHODS FOR GROUNDWATER

It's IMPORTANT TO LOCATE A water source when you are in the field, but you must also figure out how to disinfect that water. From packing filters to boiling the water over fire, the method you choose will depend on what you have on hand and how contaminated the water might be. It is not safe to ingest water that has not been disinfected.

COARSE FILTER

Coarse filtering will only remove particulate turbidity, but this should be the first step in your disinfection methods. Straining water collected in a water bottle through a bandanna is considered coarse filtering, but filters like a Millbank bag are more effective and can hold more water for multiple containers. These bags can be washed in a machine after trips and reused for the life of the fabric.

Millbank Bag

BOILING

Boiling water will kill pathogens like bacteria and viruses, but it will not remove chemicals or heavy metals. If you think your water source may contain these types of materials, use a ceramic or charcoal filter.

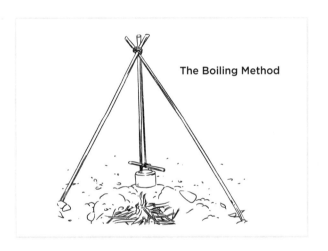

The Boiling Method

MECHANICAL FILTER

Mechanical filters come in several varieties, including pump-style, squeeze-through, and pressure filters (found in Grayl water purifier bottles), and all of these will have some type of ceramic or charcoal filter. When shopping for a mechanical filter, be sure to read the specs on each product, as some remove more materials than others, and some do not remove viruses. Boiling after filtering will always be the safest method, but many filters are 99.9% effective as a stand-alone system.

Grayl Filter

CHEMICALS

There are several chemicals that can render some contaminants inert, including plain iodine and chlorine dioxide tabs, but it pays to do some research to understand how effective they are and how they may affect your health, depending on the chemical. Then decide for yourself if they are something you wish to add to your kit.

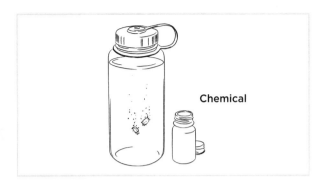

Chemical

UV LIGHT

An ultraviolet device like a SteriPEN uses UV light to render certain contaminants inert but will not remove chemicals or many viruses, so it is recommended that you research the product before use. If you decide that the water in your area is fairly safe, this may be an option for you.

UV Light

— Chapter 6 —

NAVIGATION AND SIGNALING

THERE ARE SEVERAL ASPECTS OF navigation that will aid you in an emergency. Knowing how to follow a travel **bearing** is critical. If you are unable to walk a straight line, you will have to wait for help; even if you are capable of walking out, you may chance getting lost. While this book does not teach the basic levels of navigation, it does provide those with a basic knowledge the necessary tools to enhance their skills. This chapter will cover the basics as a review.

5 BASIC NAVIGATION LESSONS WITH A COMPASS

THE REASONS FOR CARRYING A compass are varied and not as obvious as one might assume. General direction finding, which some people think is a compass's primary purpose, does not require a compass; you can use the sun for that. The most important reason to carry a compass is so that you can walk a straight line, or avoid **lateral drift**. In addition, your compass will be important when you are navigating and orienting yourself in the wilderness.

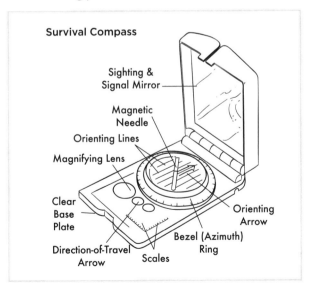

Survival Compass

Sighting & Signal Mirror

Magnetic Needle

Orienting Lines

Magnifying Lens

Clear Base Plate

Orienting Arrow

Direction-of-Travel Arrow

Scales

Bezel (Azimuth) Ring

LATERAL DRIFT

Everyone experiences lateral drift. This means that you cannot walk a straight line over a distance unless you keep sight of an object you are walking toward. Once you can no longer see your target, the body takes over and starts to move to the left or the right. Lateral drift can be accentuated by many things, like one leg that is slightly longer than the other, an unevenly loaded backpack, or walking on the side of a hill. Most people have a natural drift to the left or right, and it pays to understand how your body moves in case you need to walk a straight line during your time in the woods.

MAGNETIC NORTH

All compass needles point to magnetic north rather than true north. As long as you are not matching the compass to a printed map to plan a route, you do not need to make any adjustments to factor in magnetic **declination,** which is the difference between magnetic north and true north. The orienting arrow on the moving bezel ring is the key feature of using the compass as a navigational tool to eliminate lateral drift. If the compass is pointed in the desired direction of travel and the arrow is rotated directly under the north side of the magnetic needle (this is called "needle in the doghouse"), then you can walk a straight line, as long as the needle remains in the doghouse.

NAVIGATION AND SIGNALING

> **BUSHCRAFT TIP**
>
> The needle on your compass will always point north, so if you move the bezel ring to line up the outline, or "doghouse," so the needle is inside it, your bearing will be at the top of your compass. If you lower your compass and keep the north needle within the line in the bezel ring as you walk, you will be walking a straight line.

LEAPFROGGING

Trying to watch the compass as you walk may not be safe, in which case you'll need to leapfrog. To do this, you will use the bearing you just plugged in to sight a nearby object that you can walk toward without losing sight of it. Once you reach the object, pick another point on the same bearing and walk to it, and so on, until you get where you want to go. Once you understand leapfrogging over a distance, you are ready to move on to more advanced navigational skills.

TRAVEL BEARINGS

Your travel bearing is the number between 0 and 359 degrees that is at the top of the compass when the needle is in the doghouse. If you are given a bearing instead of choosing an object yourself, simply place the bearing at the top of the compass and then move your body until the needle is in the doghouse. You are now facing that travel bearing.

REVERSE AZIMUTH

If you become disoriented, you should first try to return to the last known point of origin, or where you came from. If you are following a travel bearing, this is as simple as looking at the bottom of the compass dial 180 degrees from your travel bearing; this will tell you the reverse **azimuth**. Dial that number to the top of the compass, put the needle back in the doghouse, and follow the new heading back to the point of origin. The more complicated way to figure out this back bearing, or reverse azimuth, is to add or subtract 180 degrees from the current travel bearing. If the travel bearing is less than 180 degrees, you add 180. If the travel bearing is greater than 180 degrees, you subtract 180 to get the reverse azimuth number.

5 INTERMEDIATE MAP NAVIGATION CONCEPTS

IN ADDITION TO YOUR COMPASS, your map is a very important tool in helping you navigate and traverse the wilderness. Learning how to properly use your map and additional navigation tools will help you plan your way before you leave, address any necessary changes that must be made at your site, and achieve a level of safety that would not exist without these skills.

DECLINATION

Simply put, declination is the difference between magnetic north on a compass and grid north. It is listed as a number of degrees in the legend of the map and could be east or west, depending on your location. If your compass has an adjustable declination, you will need to adjust it to match against a printed map before using it for navigation.

ORIENTING MAPS TO THE TERRAIN

Once your declination is set but before you can plan a route using your compass on the map or match the terrain in front of you to the map, you must orient the map. Lay the map on a flat surface (free of magnetic interferences), and place your compass in a corner of the map. Be sure that 360 is at the top of your compass, then rotate the map until the needle is in the doghouse (this will not be at 360 degrees, since you have adjusted the compass for local declination). At this point, the map is oriented to the ground, and the terrain is in front of you.

PACE COUNTING

Pace counting is the way you can track how far you have traveled. This is very important if you have a known distance to a target location, but it can also help you figure out how far you can walk in a certain amount of time. Most people walk about 3 kilometers per hour—unless they are in a hurry or the terrain is rough—so you can use this guideline to figure out approximately how long you have been walking. Since it is difficult to track paces without counting into the hundreds and thousands, you can transfer rocks from one pocket to the other or use a set of **pace beads**. Pace beads are a type of abacus on cordage. The key is knowing how many paces it takes for you to walk 100 meters. You will average this number by checking it in different terrains and up or down hills in the gear you plan to use when hiking. Once you know the number, you can count to the 100-meter pace each time and then move a pace bead (or transfer a rock or whatever method you use to track) at least ten times to get to 1 kilometer. Extra beads on another string can represent kilometers (most sets use four so that 5 kilometers of walking can be tracked).

WAYPOINTS

A waypoint is similar to the last known point of origin, except you create the waypoint before leaving that point to possibly investigate the area and plan your next move. The best way to do this is to tie something highly visible (for example, an orange shemagh) to an object in your current line of travel. Then you can go anywhere in any direction to plan your next change in travel bearing, as long as you never lose sight of the waypoint, or last known point of origin.

TERRAIN ASSOCIATION (ROUTE PLANNING)

Understanding what you are looking at on a map and identifying possible travel routes ahead of time make things much easier on the ground. The following information about maps will help you with this, but being able to see in two dimensions and imagine in three dimensions will take some practice. Your route planning will benefit greatly if you can identify areas to travel with fewer changes in elevation and minimal danger areas.

5 MAP COLORS

Colors on a map are your first clues to identifying various features and types of terrain, especially when they are combined with terrain features.

- Red = major roads
- Black = minor roads and trails (sometimes dotted lines)
- Brown = contour lines and elevation numbers
- Blue = water
- Green = vegetation; the darker the green, the heavier the vegetation

5 MAJOR TERRAIN FEATURES

Terrain features appear as brown lines on a map; the closer the lines are, the steeper the terrain. Most maps use a counter interval of about 20 meters, so every line represents an increase or decrease in elevation of 20 meters. On hilltops, a number in brown represents meters above sea level. When you look at a map, you are looking at a two-dimensional image that represents three dimensions on the ground. Contours and terrain features tell this story.

HILLTOP

Hilltops are the highest point of elevation on a rise, offering opportunities for overlooking.

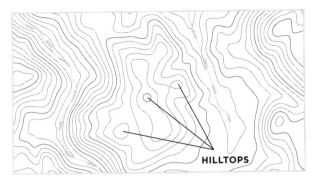

A Hilltop on a Map

SADDLE

A **saddle** is a low area between two hilltops. These areas offer good windbreak for camps without sacrificing elevation.

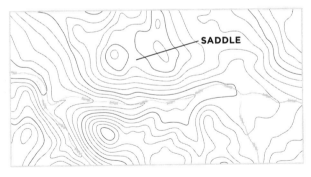

A Saddle on a Map

RIDGE

A ridge is a series of hilltops. These areas are conducive to ground travel.

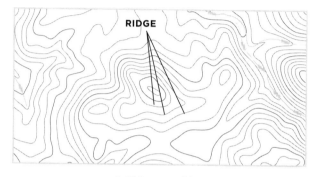

A Ridge on a Map

VALLEY

A valley is a low elevation running between ridgelines. These areas hold runoff and are the best places to look for unmarked streams. They can also be good trapping locations.

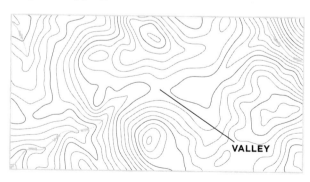

A Valley on a Map

DRAW

A **draw** is formed by two ridges with low ground between them. It is depicted on maps with U- or V-shaped contour lines.

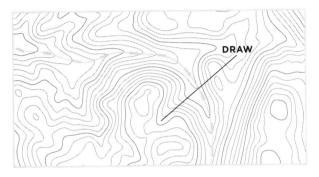

A Draw on a Map

5 MINOR TERRAIN FEATURES

In addition to the five major terrain features, these five features of a topographical map will give you a better understanding of the landscape you are traversing. It's important to be able to visualize what the area looks like in real life, and these minor features help complete that picture.

DEPRESSION

A depression is a sunken area at a lower level than the surrounding area.

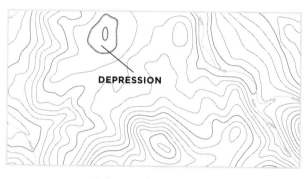

A Depression on a Map

SPUR

A spur is a short ridge jutting from another ridge.

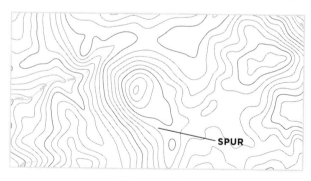

A Spur on a Map

CLIFF

A cliff is a vertical drop-off in elevation.

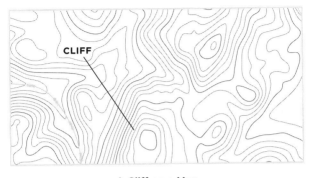

A Cliff on a Map

CUT

A cut is a humanmade passage made through raised ground for a railroad or highway.

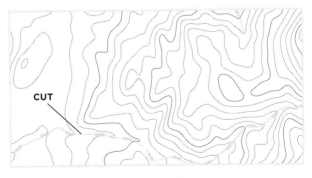

A Cut on a Map

FILL

A fill occurs when a low-level area is filled in and raised to the surrounding elevation.

A Fill on a Map

5 ADDITIONAL NAVIGATION TOOLS

ONCE YOU KNOW WHAT YOU ARE looking at, you can use some additional tools to make navigation easier.

BACKSTOPS

Backstops are points you know you should not go beyond. These are generally linear land features that run perpendicular to your intended destination. A backstop could be a river, stream, roadbed, or railway. It does not have to be right on top of your intended destination, but it will be close enough that you'll know, if you hit that feature, you have passed your mark.

HANDRAILS

Handrails are linear objects within the terrain that you can use as a guide line to follow when they lead in the intended direction of travel. A creek bed, ridgeline, river, or roadbed could all serve this function. Handrails help you navigate to a location without having to follow a compass bearing.

AIMING OFF

Aiming off is usually done in conjunction with a **baseline**. You will purposely take a bearing left or right of the intended destination a few degrees, so that you know to turn left or right to arrive at your desired location.

ESCAPE AZIMUTH

Escape azimuths are created so that if you get lost, you have a bearing to immediately plug into your compass that will take you to a known point. Say you are traveling north, and off to the east is a river that is not part of your intended travel route and is not a handrail. If you get lost, you know that a direct west azimuth from the river will take you back toward your intended course. From there, you can use that azimuth as a baseline to get your bearing for travel or to get back on track.

ATTACK POINT

Attack points are obvious features on the way to your final destination that you can aim toward easily, like a lake, trail intersection, landform, or change in terrain type. These allow you to reach your checkpoint destination easily and quickly without having to check your bearings. Once you reach the attack point, you can slow your pace and monitor your bearing as you make your way to your final destination.

— Chapter 7 —

BIND CRAFT

THE ABILITY TO TIE A variety of knots allows you to do many things in the wild. You can build shelter. You can construct tools and objects for your campsite. You can carry large loads of lumber and supplies. You can create fishing lines and game traps. An understanding and mastery of bind craft cuts down on the items you need to pack and opens up a number of opportunities for you to work with what the land makes available. The knots, hitches, and lashings described in this chapter are the essential foundation for successful bind craft. While there are many different knots one can master, this chapter makes the most out of a few types.

5 BASIC KNOTS AND HITCHES

THE BEST THING YOU CAN DO IN ANY short-term scenario is to conserve your resources, and this includes the cordage you are carrying. It is for this reason that you should use knots and hitches that are easily released for recovering and reusing your cordage materials. The following list describes several types of knots to help you build and manufacture almost anything you need in the short term.

MARLINE SPIKE HITCH

One of the most versatile of all the tools in your bind craft toolbox is the marline spike hitch. The marline spike hitch was traditionally used to attach a toggle or spike to a rope for pulling to give a better mechanical advantage. However, the usefulness of this knot is limited only to the imagination. Some examples in and around camp are a quick way to:

- Hang a pack or jacket off the ground
- Suspend a pot over the fire
- Hold tent stakes for guy lines
- Use with a frapping stick for tightening lashings or rope ladders

You will find yourself using this more than almost any other hitch when you get used to it. When pulled completely down without an attached spike or toggle, it becomes a slip loop used in the rope tackle for tightening a ridgeline.

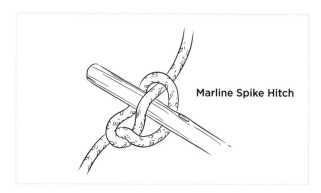

Marline Spike Hitch

BOWLINE KNOT

There are many reasons to add a loop on the end of a line for uses around and in camp as well as on the fly, and the bowline knot retains most of the rope's strength when tied. It is also easy to break it open to untie it when you are finished with it, even when it is under great pressure. It is a mainstay for your bind craft toolbox, and it is the only end-of-the-line loop I use other than a bight in the line wrapped over an object for a hitch of some sort.

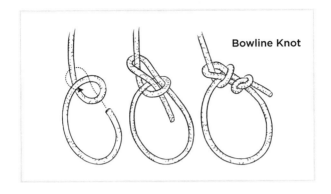

Bowline Knot

HALF HITCH

The half hitch is convenient for many tasks, including temporarily securing the end of a hitch or creating lashing, or using it to make ladders with two long poles and several rounds cut as runners. Making the loops slippery by pulling a loop of line through and not the entire tail makes them easy to untie. Half-hitch knots should be used whenever possible and safe.

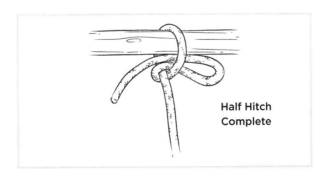

Half Hitch Complete

PRUSIK HITCH

This knot is particularly handy for attaching a loop to a line that needs to be movable along the line but that locks in a linear direction under tension. I use it for supporting tarps on a ridgeline, but it can also be used as a safety loop for ascending a rope or crossing a swift water area.

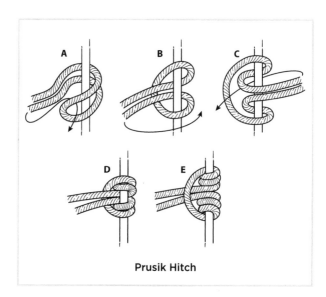

Prusik Hitch

FISHERMAN'S KNOT

This knot is useful for connecting one piece of line to create a loop. It will self-lock under strain, but it comes loose if you need to reuse the cordage. It is also known as the "necklace knot" and can be used to adjust the size of a loop to be hung around the neck in necklace fashion. I use this for creating Prusik loops.

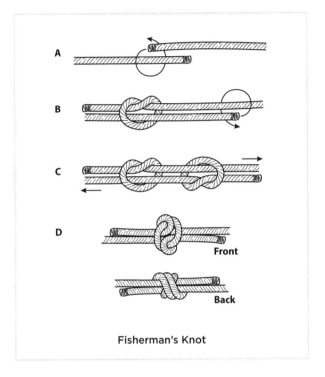

Fisherman's Knot

1

2

3

4

5

6

7

8

9

5 ADDITIONAL KNOTS

THIS NEXT SET OF KNOTS is useful for a variety of tasks. As we work with a number of knots, hitches, bends, and lashings, it's important to remember the difference between them. A knot is something that's tied within a single rope. A hitch is something that attaches a rope to an inanimate object. A bend is something that connects rope to rope. A lashing is something that connects two objects.

DOUBLE OVERHAND STOP KNOT

The double overhand stop knot is made at the end of the line. This gives the line more bulk and weight, which is helpful if you need to throw the line. It also gives the line more stopping power if you want to stop it from pulling through something.

Double Overhand Stop Knot

SLIP KNOT

The slip knot is used as a rope tackle, and can take the place of a carabiner. It's easy to come undone, and allows you to recover your cordage easily.

REEF KNOT

The reef knot is good for connecting two ropes together. It can be made by a loop-to-loop connection. It can be used to improvise netting.

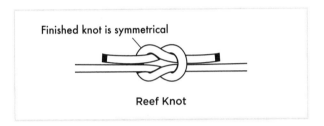

Finished knot is symmetrical

Reef Knot

SHEET BEND

The sheet bend is a great knot for joining two ropes of equal diameter when loops are not available on the end of the lines. It can also be used to improvise a hammock with a tarp or blanket.

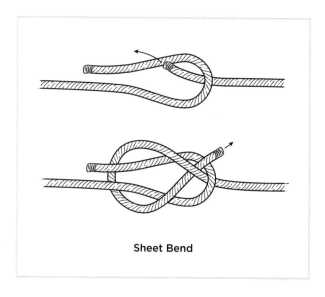

Sheet Bend

LARK'S HEAD

This knot is quick and can be used to perpendicularly attach rope to another line. This knot works very well when attaching cords to a line for the purpose of weaving or hanging something from them. You can even use this type of knot for toggles when you are not able to double over the line or when you simply need to hang a single line.

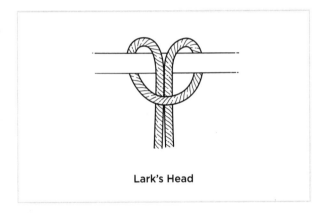

Lark's Head

5 LASHINGS

Lashings are wraps of cordage that are used to carry some type of weight or to support an object or structure. From camp furniture to different types of shelters, lashings are required to make them strong.

ROUND LASH

Starting with a timber hitch and ending with a clove hitch, round lashes are used to connect two poles for increasing length. This requires no frappings, only wrapping.

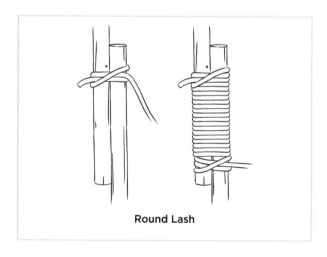

Round Lash

SHEAR LASH

A shear lashing is used to make a bipod from two poles and involves frapping wraps between the two poles as a pivot point.

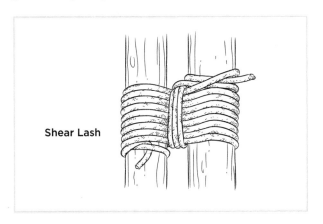

Shear Lash

TRIPOD LASH

The tripod lash is similar to the shear lash, except three poles are used with frapping between each of the pivots.

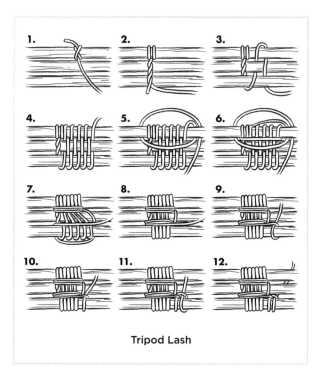

1. **2.** **3.**

4. **5.** **6.**

7. **8.** **9.**

10. **11.** **12.**

Tripod Lash

SQUARE LASH

Square lashings can be done with or without frapping, depending on whether you have notched the materials. When the material is notched, you don't need frappings to lock anything in place because the notch performs that function. This lashing is used when rounds are to be lashed at 90-degree angles to each other.

BIND CRAFT

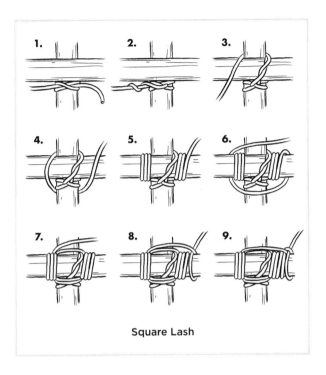

Square Lash

DIAGONAL LASH

Diagonal lashings are similar to square lashings, but they form an X pattern over the two components generally used when rounds are at angles other than 90 degrees. Again, frappings are dictated by whether notches are used. Diagonal lashes can be used for 90-degree components for extra security or if you don't need a flat finish to the piece.

1. **2.**

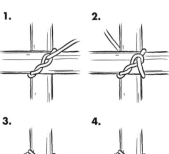

3. **4.**

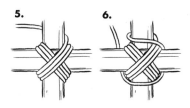

5. **6.**

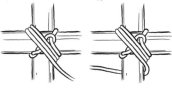

7. **8.**

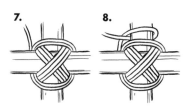

Diagonal Lash

CORDAGE MANAGEMENT

MOST PEOPLE CARRY CORDAGE of some sort in their everyday kits. This is one of the 5Cs because it is time consuming to create cordage with a high enough tensile strength from landscape materials. Personally, I carry only two types of cordage most of the time and add a third (rope) if the outing calls for it. I divide my cordage into two categories: expendable (cordage that can be cut into small pieces as necessary for different projects) and nonexpendable (cordage typically used as a whole that I want to recover easily). The best choice for expendable cordage is bank line, and the best choice for nonexpendable cordage is paracord. Bank line is meant to be used for semipermanent projects or something quickly needed, so I don't worry about cutting it to an exact length or trying to recover it. With paracord, on the other hand, I prefer to cut it to a certain length one time and then use it over and over for other tasks.

One thing to consider ahead of time is cordage management. When you are in the field, you want things to be as easy as possible. I suggest cutting nine pieces of 550 paracord at 7' each and then tying a bowline knot on one end and a stop knot on the other. You can store most of this in your kit, but you should keep one piece in your pocket for emergencies. For expendable cordage, I suggest having at least 100' of bank line on hand, which you can use for extra lashings and shelter building for emergencies or repairs, first aid, and so on.

— Chapter 8 —

LANDSCAPE RESOURCES (TREES)

WHEN IT COMES TO TREES, the first thing to remember is that they are a four-season resource unless you are using nuts or leaves from a deciduous species. But for construction materials, fire starting, and most medicines, trees are a great resource in all four seasons. The one exception may be containers made from bark, which are always best made in the spring when the sap is running and the bark separates easily from the sapwood. I call trees a *critical resource*, as almost everything you need can be manufactured from them. From fire and tools to shelters and medicine—if you understand the various species in the eastern woodlands, you will have what you need. Understanding how to process these materials for use is also a very important aspect when it comes to using them to their fullest potential. The following sections will discuss what to use and how to process it in an emergency situation.

5 USEFUL TREES (BASIC LEVEL)

I WILL NOT TRY TO EXPLAIN ALL THE USES and resources that can be taken or used from each of these five trees, but I will provide a base of knowledge that you can use quickly and easily in the case of short-term survival.

It is worth noting that ash or coal from a burned hardwood (deciduous) tree has many medicinal and hygienic benefits. Ash is antiseptic and styptic (can stop bleeding); it makes a good dry shampoo or foot powder as well. Charcoal has long been used to absorb toxins and as a drying agent, so it can be used for suspected poisoning or a festering wound. Charcoal is a great addition to your personal first aid kit that you are creating incidentally from a campfire.

PINE

In the eastern woodlands, you should concern yourself only with red or white pine. White pines have five (think five letters in the word "white") needles in a cluster. Red pines have two needles in a cluster.

White Pine

FIRE

Pine trees contain volatile oils that burn very hot. Certain areas of the tree, generally where there is a branch junction on the trunk or in the roots of a standing or fallen dead tree, are full of this oil known as "fatwood" or "lighter wood." This wood is a fantastic fire-starting tinder when processed to fine material shavings or when sawed into to create dust. Dry branches and needles will catch fire quickly with open flame and make good kindling material.

SHELTER

Large species of pine with large lower branches can be used as a quick shelter to temporarily protect you from snow and rain.

WATER

Pines are a great resource when you need to disinfect water quickly because the volatile oils make the wood burn very hot and very fast.

SIGNALING AND NAVIGATION

If you need to create a signal fire, use green pine boughs. The pine **resin** creates a black smoke that will be easy to see, and the oils cause the wood to burn quickly.

SELF-AID

The sap from red and white pines is highly antiseptic, with white being the better for this purpose. Pine sap can be used to plug a lost tooth filling or cover an exposed nerve from a broken tooth. Using pine sap as a dressing works well for abrasions. Pine needles are high in vitamin C, which make a great immune system booster when used in an infusion.

TULIP POPLAR

The tulip poplar is the tallest tree in the eastern woodlands, growing to 60' to 90'. Because of its height, it is fairly easy to identify from a distance; close-up, it can be recognized by its large, lobed leaf. It was called "mother in law's night shirt" in colonial times. It was a favorite wood for carving and provides many resources to use for your survival priorities.

Tulip Poplar

FIRE

The tulip poplar is a choice wood for bow drill fires, and the inner bark can be processed into fine material for tinder.

SHELTER

A softer hardwood with long, straight trunks, these trees make excellent shelter material where longer poles are needed.

SELF-AID

Due to its heavy tannin content, tulip poplar is a good drawing agent for topical use and is also used on sprains and bruising. For internal use, you can make infusions from its leaves and flowers and decoctions from the inner bark. Drinking a decoction of tulip poplar will cause you to sweat thereby raising your core body temperature. The inner bark and especially the roots make a highly acrid decoction traditionally used as a stimulant and digestive tonic. During warm months, the outer bark separates easily from the sapwood and can be used to make a large splint. You can use the inner bark to make a smaller splint.

ASPEN

The aspen is a true poplar, whereas the tulip poplar is actually a magnolia. This fact aside, the trees are very similar in most aspects, which is probably how the tulip poplar got its name. All the information in the tulip poplar entry applies to the aspen as well, but there are two important differences in terms of resource usage.

1. The first is that the aspen's inner bark is a bit more coarse than the tulip poplar's. This means that the aspen may require more processing for fire tinder materials if you're relying on an ember for ignition.
2. The second difference is that aspen turns to punky wood much more efficiently than tulip poplar and is the best resource for making charred materials. If you find good dry punk from this tree, you can create a solar-generated ember without charring.

The aspen's medicinal properties are similar to those of the willow (see 5 Additional Apothecary Trees (Intermediate) in this chapter), as the bark contains salicin, which is used for pain relief.

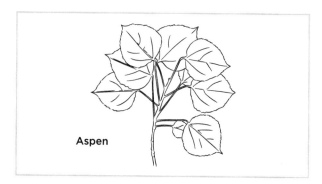

Aspen

BIRCH

There are many species of birch, and all are effective in the realm of fire starting due to their volatile oils. Some species contain higher concentrations of this oil and are more effective.

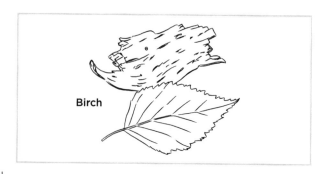

Birch

FIRE

White and yellow birch are preferred, but in some parts of the eastern woodlands, river birch may be the only option. River birch—or black birch, as it is also known—does not have as high a concentration of volatile oils, but it can be processed to increase surface area and will take the spark from a ferrocerium rod or work very well with open flame.

SHELTER

Some birch species have barks that can be cut from the trees to create large sheets used for roofing or for covering a shelter.

WATER

You can tap and extract consumable liquid straight from the birch. It may take several hours to fill a container, but it can be done. Birch species like the river birch get their name because they grow close to water and in very wet soils. For this reason, they are water indicator trees.

SELF-AID

There is a lot of lore about native uses of the birch tree, but actual documentation for common ailments is hard to find. However, there is plenty written about the use of extracted birch oils as a liniment for aching muscles and joints.

HICKORY

The mighty hickory is a pioneering species if ever there was one in the eastern woodlands. Its wood rivals the strongest synthetic materials for making tool handles of all types. For our purposes, its properties of strength and flexibility make it perfect for many building tasks.

Hickory

FIRE

Hickory has a BTU (British thermal unit) of 27.7, second only to osage, making it a premium long-burning and hot wood for a fire that needs to last the night without too much fuss.

SHELTER

Due to their strength and flexibility, hickory saplings of 4" make fantastic ridge beams when shelter building and excellent supports for freestanding structures as well. The bast (the fiber extracted after soaking the bark) of the hickory is said to be one of the strongest materials for making natural cordage.

5 ADDITIONAL APOTHECARY TREES (INTERMEDIATE)

NATURAL RESOURCES ARE AN ESSENTIAL component of bushcraft. Trees are especially useful because they are accessible throughout all four seasons. From being a fuel source to helping with navigation, different trees have many different uses. They also provide a bounty of natural remedies. These five trees in particular are extremely helpful for survival.

OAK

As with pines, you only need to consider the red or white variety of oaks. The easiest way to identify these common species is to look at the leaves in season or on the ground near the tree. The leaves of red oaks have points on the lobes, and those of the white oak are rounded. Think about a point being sharp, and sharp will draw blood, so points are red oak. If you cannot find or easily recognize leaves among the forest debris, look at the inner bark: The red oak has red bark, and the white oak has white bark.

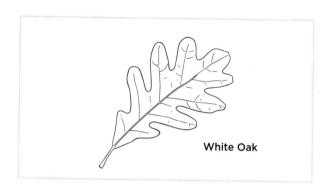

White Oak

FIRE

Hardwoods like oaks have long, close fibers, which means they burn very hot, making them good for long campfires and for producing coals for cooking. Different woods have different BTU values. White oak has a BTU of 24, and a softer wood like white pine has a BTU of only 15.9. Wood with a higher BTU will burn hotter and longer.

SHELTER

Structural integrity is an important consideration when building a frame or a more advanced natural shelter. With hardwoods, especially green hardwoods like oak, you can trust even a 4"-diameter log used as a ridge to support quite a bit of weight while still maintaining some flexibility due to the long fibers. The inner bark of these trees can also be split to create makeshift withies or **bindings** to conserve your cordage.

WATER

Oak produces long-burning fires if you need to boil large amounts of water. This is a great fire-sustaining wood for fuel.

SELF-AID

White oaks provide valuable antiseptic, anti-inflammatory, and astringent remedies. The inner bark is the most valuable resource for medicinal use. The bark should be made into a decoction if ingested and can also be ground and used raw or moist for external use. A decoction can be taken internally for diarrhea or gargled for a sore throat.

WILLOW

There are several species of willow in the United States. White willow has the most resources for medicinal use, but all willows can be used in some way for most survival priorities.

Willow

FIRE

Although this is technically a hardwood (deciduous) species, its wood is soft and, combined with a long-fibered inner bark, is great for fire starting. This tree truly gives you all the elements needed for a good fire and is one of the best species to use for a bow drill fire. The inner bark can be broken down for bird's nests or tinder bundles; the smaller dead branches will combust quickly, making a good kindling; and the larger logs will create a decent intermediate fuel until harder woods can be added.

SHELTER

Withies are made from willow. Small green shoots make excellent bindings to conserve cordage.

WATER

Willow is a water indicator tree and generally grows close to ponds, creeks, and streams, so being able to identify it from a distance will generally lead you to a groundwater resource.

SIGNALING AND NAVIGATION

As stated, willows generally grow near water, so if you are navigating to a water source from a distance, a willow can lead you there.

SELF-AID

Willow bark was first used as a mild painkiller and later synthesized to create aspirin, so a decoction of the inner bark can be used for this purpose. The inner bark from this tree can also be removed to make improvised splints.

BLACK WALNUT

Black walnut grows in dark, rich soil, but it can be scarce in many areas due to overharvesting. It was one of the most prized woods in colonial times for everything from gunstocks and furniture to fenceposts, so this tells you it has great strength when used for construction.

Black Walnut

FIRE

With a value of 20 BTUs, black walnut is an average heat generator for a warming fire, and because it is a harder wood, its burning longevity makes it very good for an all-night fire as well.

WATER

Even though iodine is used to disinfect groundwater resources, the concentration of iodine that can be derived from a decoction of black walnut has not been studied, so it is unknown how it compares with a viable disinfection method like the 2 percent tincture of iodine available commercially.

SELF-AID

The black walnut has three main chemical compounds, two of which are tannin (astringent) and iodine (antiseptic). The greatest source of iodine comes from the green nut hulls, which can be ground and decocted to release the iodine.

A 1-ounce serving of black walnuts contains:

- Calories: 170
- Protein: 7 grams
- Fat: 17 grams
- Carbs: 3 grams
- Fiber: 2 grams
- Magnesium: 14% of the RDI
- Phosphorus: 14% of the RDI
- Potassium: 4% of the RDI
- Iron: 5% of the RDI
- Zinc: 6% of the RDI
- Copper: 19% of the RDI
- Manganese: 55% of the RDI
- Selenium: 7% of the RDI

RDI = Reference Daily Intake
www.healthline.com/nutrition/black-walnut#nutrition

DOGWOOD

Dogwood grows in most areas on the edges of the eastern woodlands. Flowering dogwood has a white to pinkish flower in the summer, and has a dark and heavily segregated bark. It grows very twisted—never straight. Often it will lean toward a clearing or field edge, and generally has a low crown.

Dogwood

FIRE

Since dogwood is very dense, it will burn for a long time. It also produces very high-quality coals, but does not produce a lot of smoke.

SELF-AID

Dogwood has astringent, analgesic, and anti-inflammatory properties. For self-aid, you can use dogwood to help treat fever and chills, headaches, and diarrhea. Historically, dogwood was used to help treat malaria.

SWEETGUM

Sweetgum is a deciduous tree found in the southeastern United States as well as parts of Mexico and Central America. Its leaves typically have five sharp lobes. It is recognizable by its spiny seed-carrying fruit.

Sweetgum

SELF-AID

The most usable part of this tree for self-aid is the sap that seeps from it when it is damaged, although you can extract this powerful compound (storax) from a decoction of the inner bark. The sap, however, will yield this compound only through an infusion. Sweetgum has long been used in such infusions and decoctions as a tea to relieve cough and cold symptoms.

1

2

3

4

5

6

7

8

9

MEDICINAL PREPS

UNDERSTANDING AND USING THE medicinal remedies that can be derived from trees and plants is an advanced but important skill. Just like understanding how to harvest material to create usable objects, making medicinals from the landscape can greatly aid you in a long-term situation and can make the short term more bearable depending on your issue. Medicinals are a helpful addition to your first aid kit (FAK) and can be combined with other kit items to treat common ailments like bleeding, inflammation, upset stomach, and so on. There is a bit more to using herbal remedies than you may realize. It is usually not as simple as just grabbing something and eating it or rubbing it on your skin, although sometimes that can be enough. With most of the trees discussed here, you will need to use the inner bark, roots, nutshells, and so on, which involves extracting the medicinal components in easy-to-learn processes. Once you understand a few simple processes, you can harness the healing power of the trees around you.

RAW

Using an herbal component (known as "mark") in its raw form means you can simply use it in its harvested state, whether that is eating it as a raw food source, rubbing it on a wound, or placing it directly on a wound to be bandaged and held in place.

INFUSION

An infusion is a simple tea. The mark is macerated and steeped in preboiled water for about 10–15 minutes. The liquid is then strained and used as a wash, fomentation, or drink. Infusions are made with leaves and flowers but *not* the woody parts of trees or nut hulls. Infusions and decoctions can be made with less liquid to use as a **poultice**. The resulting liquid is not only useful as a tea but can also be used to wash a wound or as a fomentation.

DECOCTION

A decoction is made with the woody parts of trees and plants like roots, barks, stems, and so on. To create a decoction, you boil the mark instead of steeping it. It is best to boil a decoction until half the starting amount of water has evaporated during the process.

POULTICE

A poultice involves wetting the mark in some way and placing it directly on the affected area. There are three types of poultices. A spit poultice is made on the fly by chewing the mark, mixing it with your saliva, and then placing it. It is important to chew the mark thoroughly. The other two types are hot

1
2
3
4
5
6
7
8
9

and cold poultices, which are generally created by macerating the mark and creating a shallow decoction, then removing the mark and using that for the treatment.

FOMENTATION

A fomentation is the process of warming an area of the body and keeping it moist; this is done to reduce inflammation or dissipate bruising. You can create a fomentation by making a decoction or infusion and then soaking a piece of cotton or other natural material in the solution, then wrapping it around the affected area.

— Chapter 9 —

PIONEERING

THE MORE TIME YOU SPEND in the woods, the more things you will need to accomplish and build. This chapter will teach you about a few simple tools and techniques that can help you accomplish your goals without having to carry too many implements with you.

5 SIMPLE MACHINES OF SURVIVAL IMPORTANCE

THESE FIVE MACHINES CAN BE EASILY crafted out of the materials you have packed as well as wood material you are able to forage. Each one is meant to help with life around camp and can aid in outdoor survival. From helping to set up and fortify camp to starting fire, these machines may be simple, but their output is extremely beneficial.

ROPE TACKLE

A rope tackle is used to tighten a standing rope. It can be used to put tension on a simple ridgeline for a shelter or to tighten a rope used by a group to cross fast-moving water. A rope tackle is made with a simple slip knot with the loop pulled taut toward the working end of the line. This loop is the same loop used for a marline spike, but instead of placing a toggle or spike in the line, you simply want to pass a loop through the working end to use like a pulley to put tension on the standing end.

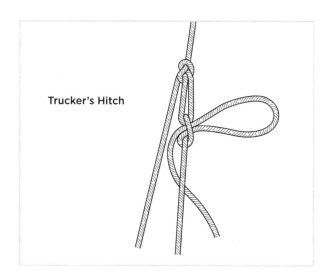

Trucker's Hitch

WINDLASS

A windlass is a twisting of the rope with a toggle, like with a tourniquet. A windlass can be made with a loop of cord or rope anchored to a fixed object and then looped around another object. A simple example of this is its use on a bucksaw: The loop of rope goes over the uprights, and a toggle is used in the middle to twist the rope, providing tension, and then it is locked off on the crossbar of the saw. This could be done on a larger scale to bring down a standing dead tree or even to drag a log over some distance. The windlass could also be increased in size and used with a T handle for aid in turning, but the concept is the same.

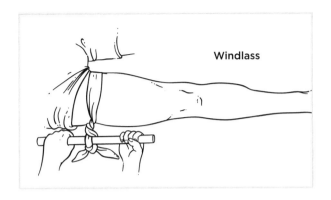

Windlass

BOW/DRILL

The simple bow-and-drill machine has been used for centuries for everything from boring holes to igniting an ember. It is an excellent example of a simple machine that is adaptable to many applications. Making the bow is as simple as tying a string to a branch. There are many complicated notches and holes you can create to string the bow, but I recommend a simple fork on one end of the stick with a loop and a stake notch on the other end to tie it off with a straight lashing and a clove hitch. The string does not need to be so tight that it causes the bow to bend in order to load the drill, but the string cannot be so loose that the drill slips under downward pressure.

1

2

3

4

5

6

7

8

9

Bow/Drill

LEVER AND FULCRUM

Used for lifting heavy objects, this simple machine is one of Archimedes's inventions. By using a long lever and pivot point, you can lift objects with less force, relying instead on mechanical advantage. To get a heavy log off the ground, you could wedge a long green branch of good dimension under the log and then place a large rock or another crosscut log under this lever for a pivot point. You will be able to lift the log with less physical exertion. You could also apply the opposite principle and use a tripod from above and a lever through a loop under the tripod. By using the rope as the pivot point, you could create a type of crane device using the same method.

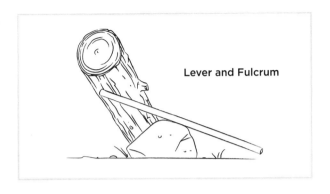
Lever and Fulcrum

INCLINE PLANE

This simple machine allows you to raise heavy objects without lifting them. You can use an incline plane to roll a large log to a bucking station, although you may also need a lever depending on the situation. This would probably be a two-person operation unless you use stakes to hold one end of a longer object in place while the other end is moved to that level. But on the whole, the inclined plane allows movement of heavy weights with much less effort.

Incline Plane

5 WOODEN TOOLS

SOME OF THE EASIEST ITEMS TO manufacture instead of carrying them are simple wooden tools. You should make these tools once you have decided that your situation requires you to stay overnight or longer. Other tools can be made as needed but will be very useful over a short time.

Whether you are in a situation that requires you to spend a night or two in the woods, or you have chosen to stay for that period, the less weight you carry, the better off you will be at making miles. Making your own simple tools will lessen the weight you have to carry. Planning the chores you may need to perform will help you understand what type of simple wooden tools you will need.

MALLET
For elementary tasks, a simple battening stick will do, especially in an emergency, but for more complicated tasks, you may need to make a mallet or even a maul. A simple mallet can be made from any round. You want to remove the stock from about half the round to create a comfortable grip. You can keep the other end as is. That heavier, full diameter of the round becomes the mallet's head. This takes less effort and will be more effective at battening your axe to split

smaller rounds, pounding stakes, and so on. A maul is just a large mallet with a longer handle, in case you need something to drive pilot hole stakes or to strike large wooden wedges to split logs.

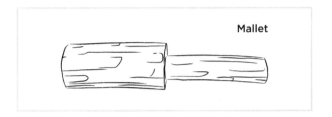

Mallet

WEDGE

Wooden wedges can be made from the material that falls off when making your mallet, or they can be created to the size needed at the time, but either way, they will come in handy when splitting wood. If your knife gets buried into a round when battening, a simple wedge will free it and then split the wood. A wedge can be used with a knife in an emergency and to avoid too much battening of the knife. If a dry wood round has a natural crack, a wedge can be used instead of other metal tools to split the wood.

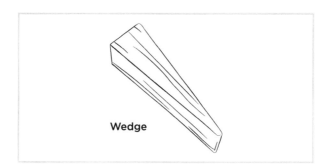

Wedge

BUCKSAW

A bucksaw is a simple tool you can create if you are already carrying a blade in your pack. The blade can be taped to the inside of a belt or placed in your axe sleeve. The ability to craft a bucksaw is useful in case something happens to the saw you may already be carrying that employs this blade type. A bucksaw can be easily made and takes advantage of the previously mentioned windlass to tension the blade between two uprights that pivot on a crossbar. There are many ways to make this tool on the fly, but the longevity of its use should dictate its construction method. Making a bucksaw from a single round if you have an axe works well, but you can make one from three simple rounds that are about 1" in diameter. The length of the blade dictates the length of the components you will make. The size of the log to be cut will dictate the crossbar distance on the uprights and the length of the uprights themselves.

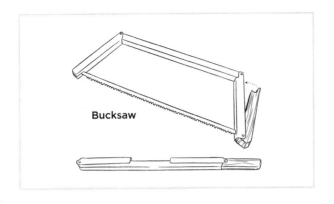

Bucksaw

TRIPOD

Tripods are useful for a myriad of tasks depending on their size and configuration, from simply suspending a pot over the fire, to creating a shelter frame, to hanging large game for processing. Tripods are one of the most useful tools in camp.

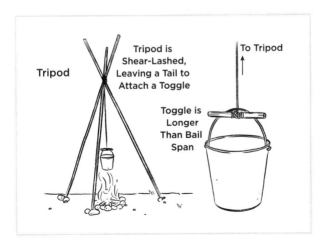

Tripod

Tripod is Shear-Lashed, Leaving a Tail to Attach a Toggle

To Tripod

Toggle is Longer Than Bail Span

PACK FRAME

Depending on the application, a pack frame can be used for hauling anything, including firewood or large game after quartering back to camp or even large water containers to and from the source. There are many different types of frames, but the standard **Roycroft or Roycraft frame** is probably the easiest and quickest one to make. For long-term use or to carry anything more than a tarp of gear, however, I find that the ladder-style or Alaskan-style frames are more durable and give a better weight distribution for heavier loads. These can be made with or without an empty shelf on the bottom. The longer the pack frame will be used, the more complex its construction should be.

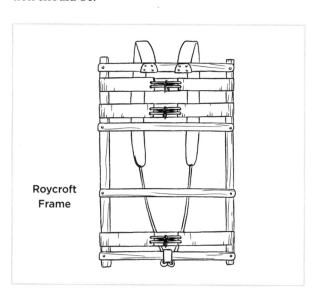

Roycroft Frame

5 CRITICAL AXE SKILLS

An axe is an important bushcraft tool because of its many uses. There are many types of axes, handles, and head weights available, and many are meant for specific purposes. You should consider how you may be using your axe while out in the woods when deciding which axe or axes to pack. These five critical skills are basic but important ways you can use your axe to help with your outdoor survival.

FELLING

Bringing a tree from standing to the ground can be tricky business, depending on the tree's size, but felling techniques are not difficult to learn, and smaller trees are fairly safe if precautions are taken. If you need to **fell** a tree, consider the following before you proceed:

1. Select the smallest available tree that will meet your needs.
2. Ensure that the safe zone is clear of any gear or obstructions. (This includes other trees that may affect the tree's fall. A tree hung halfway down in another treetop presents a whole other set of issues.)
3. Ensure that you have a good escape route from the area behind where the tree will hinge.

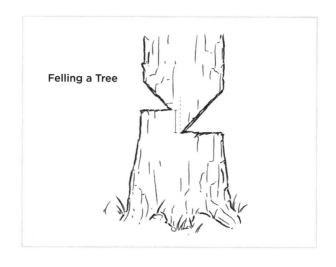

Felling a Tree

LIMBING

Removing lower limbs before bucking (see the following section) is essential and is usually done with an axe, although a saw can be used. Standing on the opposite side of the trunk and cutting in the direction of growth will make this process safer and easier. To limb a tree that is lying on the ground, always cut from the back of the limb's connection to the tree, not into the crotch or apex of the connection. Splitting into the crotch will often cause the tree to split and will not clean-cut the branch.

Limbing

BUCKING

Taking a long round and reducing it to manage-able pieces is called "bucking" the log. You can use a saw at the end of the process to create the length you want, but at the beginning, especially if you are working with a larger tree, it is easier to use an axe.

When bucking logs with an axe, use a V notch and roll the log to make four cuts, completing the separation. When cutting a notch in the log, you should stand on top of the log to make your cuts, if possible. If the log diameter is too small to stand on comfortably, stand opposite to the side you are cutting. Never make the cut on top of the log but always on the sides to avoid errant glancing strikes that could cause injury.

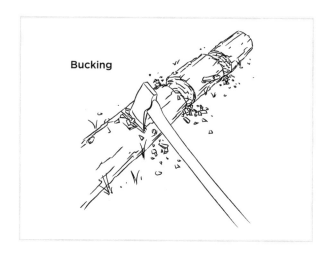

Bucking

SPLITTING

After bucking the firewood to size, you will need to split the wood. You may need to split a longer log for a project, and wedges can assist with this. Most of this work is done by axe with the help of wedges and/or mauls.

If possible, you should split firewood while kneeling to reduce the distance of the axe swing if you miss the log. Kneeling is a much safer position than standing and keeps your legs away from possible contact with the axe.

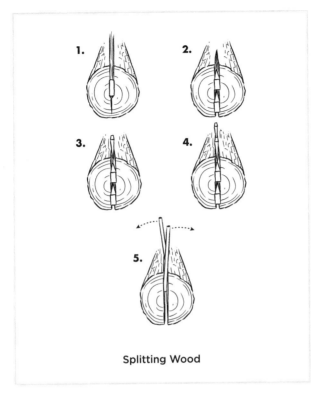

Splitting Wood

HEWING

Creating a flat surface or semi-dimensional pieces requires hewing the faces to remove irregularities like waves in grain or knots. This is called "hewing," and it is usually done with your axe, especially for smaller projects.

1

2

3

4

5

6

7

8

9

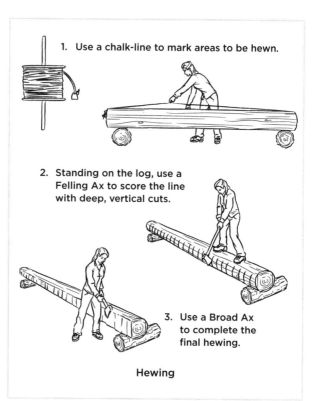

1. Use a chalk-line to mark areas to be hewn.

2. Standing on the log, use a Felling Ax to score the line with deep, vertical cuts.

3. Use a Broad Ax to complete the final hewing.

Hewing

5 TOOL RULE

No MATTER WHAT YOU DECIDE TO MAKE from wood or use it for, several methods may be necessary. With the five processes that follow, you can create anything from a spoon to a log cabin depending on the size of your materials and tools.

CROSSCUT

Crosscutting the grain is easily accomplished with a saw, but you can also use an axe in an angular fashion. This is a necessary step to bring full trees to the ground or to reduce the round to manageable lengths (bucking).

SPLIT

Splitting the wood with the grain means using the cutting tool, usually an axe or knife, on top of the end grain to split the wood, separating the fibers.

SHAPE

Shaping the wood to create a usable object means carving, and this can be accomplished with many tools, but a knife is the most common.

BORE

If you are creating holes for pegging materials together or for lashing and binding, you want a tool with a drilling function, such as an awl or a larger boring bit of some kind.

DEPRESSION MAKING (CONCAVITIES)

You can create concavities, or bowls, with embers from a fire burning the wood, but it is much safer to use a tool to keep from cracking green woods by drying them too quickly. Some sort of hook knife or mocotaugan will work best, but larger projects may require tools like a gouge or curved adze.

5 CRITICAL KNIFE SKILLS

THERE ARE MANY KNIFE-CRAFT SKILLS that are important to survival, and many overlap in some way. I created a list of topics or skills I believe to be most effective in an emergency if you are left with only your trusty sheath knife as a tool. To that end, fire and shelter will be more important to you than most other things, so the skills you must initially learn are based on this precept.

CREATING FIRE LAY MATERIALS

There are three elements of any fire lay: tinder, kindling, and fuel. With this in mind, you have to consider how to use your knife to process all three effectively and safely, while still remembering that the tool itself is a resource to be conserved as much as possible. The number one rule in conservation theory is: Don't use your knife unless you have to. Instead, look for wood that is already on the ground and that is the right size to create the kindling and fuel elements of your fire. Of course, there may not always be enough wood or usable wood, so that is when you rely on your knife. To create tinder materials, look for trees like cedars or poplars, as their inner barks are highly combustible and can be worked by hand once harvested to create a bird's nest or tinder bundle.

The bird's nest and tinder bundle are two different structures for two different purposes, but both have the same result: burning the mass that is your initial point of combustion, which will help light your increasingly larger materials of kindling and fuel. The bird's nest contains very finely processed material in the center to accept and cradle an ember like that from a bow drill fire or from charred materials. The tinder bundle is not much more than a ball of coarse material to be ignited with either open flame or a ferrocerium rod. You want to avoid, as much as possible, using the blade of your knife for this, which is why a 90-degree sharp spine (not unlike a cabinet scraper) is a helpful feature of a good knife. You can also use this 90-degree spine to shave smaller stick materials like fatwoods and softer species to create fine shavings that, in my opinion, are far superior to **feather sticks** and that have less effect on the knife, thereby conserving the blade edge.

For kindling material and fuel wood, you may need to baton the blade of your knife to split material along the grain to reduce the diameter. You may also need to baton across the grain diagonally to reduce the length if you cannot break it by hand or use the fork of a tree for leverage to snap the length. **Batoning** is a controversial subject because it can cause damage to your knife, but it is an indispensable skill if you only have a knife to process wood. There are some dos and don'ts associated with batoning. First, try to use material that is free of knots and as small in diameter as can be used comfortably, and, if possible, do not use a knife without a full tang. When you need to baton to split the grain, always try to keep initial impact blows in the center of the blade and centered in the material. Once you have split the grain, you should be able to place a wooden wedge in the split and baton that to complete the task. A good rule for splitting is to never split a log that is so large it will not allow at least an inch of the blade to protrude from the split once the knife disappears into the split. If you have to strike the knife again, strike the tip, never the handle. It is important to have some sort of anvil under the material in case the knife goes cleanly through a split, so the blade does not strike the ground or other hard materials, causing potential damage.

USING AS A FIRE-STARTING TOOL

It is important to think of your knife as a significant part of your fire-starting capability when it comes to combustion from striking the ferrocerium rod using the spine, to using as a steel for flint, and for steel ignition (a big advantage of a high-carbon steel blade).

Using the back 90-degree spine of the knife to strike a ferrocerium rod accomplishes several important and often overlooked tasks. First, you do not have to carry a separate striker of some kind (most of which are inadequate for the task anyway). You can also get much better leverage on your knife to strike the rod than with a smaller device like a cut-off hacksaw blade. It is important to understand that the true function of the ferrocerium rod is as an *emergency* ignition tool, so you want the maximum amount of material removed from the rod with a single strike (this is why I believe a soft, large rod is better than a smaller or harder rod). You can apply full power and maximize the surface area being pushed against the rod with a knife blade.

Now to the high-carbon steel aspect. Once you have made an initial emergency fire, your priority should shift to next-fire mentality, which means conserving resources by making charred material—whether from cotton material in your kit or natural material, like punky wood, fungus, or plant materials like cattail heads. You can ignite this material several ways, including striking a hard rock against the back of a high-carbon steel knife and effecting ignition and placing the ember into a bird's nest and fire lay.

CUTTING SAPLINGS

This skill is necessary for shelter building, as green wood may be preferable depending on the type of shelter you want to build. Obviously, the flexibility of green wood has distinct advantages when making dome-type structures, as well as structural integrity that may be compromised when using **deadfall** materials. Cutting a sapling is as easy as taking advantage of the tree's weakness: Simply bend the sapling, which will overstress the fibers, and cut into the fibers at an angle toward the root ball.

FELLING A TREE

When I discuss felling a tree with a knife, I am not talking about felling a fifty-year-old tree that you would typically process with an axe or axe and saw combination. I am referring to manageable sizes up to 4"–5" that you cannot just bend over and **shear cut**. For this emergency knife use, you only need to harvest material that is a large enough diameter to be used for your structure or that will make good fuel if you are harvesting a standing tree that is dead. This technique is also known as "beaver chewing" because you will baton your blade to create a V notch around the tree, steadily reducing the diameter until you can push the tree over for further use or processing.

CREATING NOTCHES

Notching material is mostly necessary for building of structures, but it can also be used for simple things like manipulating a pot over a fire, creating trap components, and making simple stakes for tarps

1

2

3

4

5

6

7

8

9

and tents. To understand the importance of notches, think about log homes; simple notches are what hold everything together without the use of nails. You may combine cord with notches to bind them more effectively, but the notch enables the interlocking of wood components. The most important yet rudimentary notches are the 7" notch, the log cabin notch, the saddle notch, the hook notch, and the V notch. With these three simple notches, many structures can be constructed.

5 SAFE KNIFE POSITIONS

IT'S ESSENTIAL TO ALWAYS HANDLE your knives safely. Practicing with your knife will make you more comfortable, but don't replace caution with complacency. A sharp knife is a double-edged sword: capable of the finest of carving tasks but also capable of inflicting a deep wound and leaving permanent damage. The last thing you want in the wilderness is to injure yourself (or anyone else) through carelessness.

FIST GRIP

Always grip your knife as if making a fist; this will not only give you leverage and control; it will also eliminate any chance of your fingers contacting the cutting surface. If you must choke up on your knife blade for a finer carving task or to use the tip of the knife, you should wear leather gloves if available.

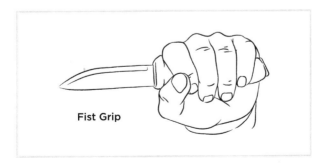

Fist Grip

CHEST LEVER

For the chest lever grip, hold the material in one hand and point the knife outward with the other. Lever both arms like chicken wings from the chest, using your back muscles to control and remove material by moving the object to be cut and the knife blade simultaneously.

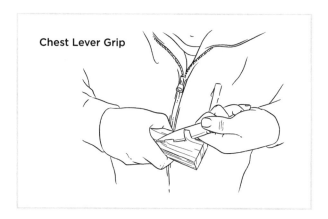

Chest Lever Grip

KNEE LEVER

For the knee lever, lock the wrist of the hand holding the knife into your opposite knee while in a kneeling position. Then draw the material toward the blade, removing material without moving the knife itself. This method is especially effective for taking off large amounts of wood, as well as for finer carving of points.

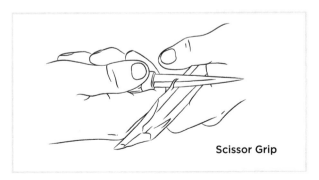
Knee Lever Grip

SCISSOR GRIP

For the scissor grip, you pivot the knife like a pair of scissors with the thumb of the hand holding the wood acting as a pivot point for the hand holding the knife. The back of the hand holding the wood acts as a stop. You can use it for very fine shavings or coarser cuts.

Scissor Grip

REVERSE GRIP THUMB SAFETY

This grip keeps your hand from sliding down onto the blade when you are pushing the knife down into something. You must keep your thumb on top of the butt of the knife and point the grind away from you.

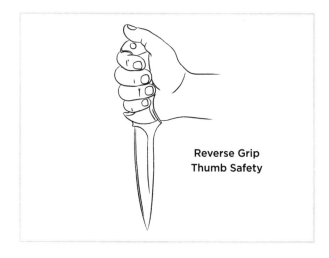

**Reverse Grip
Thumb Safety**

5 BELT KNIFE CRITERIA

THE REASONS FOR EXACTING CRITERIA when selecting a belt knife are built on years of experience in multi-functionality and ease of use. If a knife is your only tool in an emergency, it must perform well at all critical functions and be easily maintained at the same time.

FULL TANG

Full tang means there is one continuous piece of material throughout, from the blade to the end of the handle, with no reduction in the steel to create possible weak points that may hinge under stress. The scales are then pinned or sometimes bolted to the knife blank to provide an acceptable and ergonomic handle and grip.

SHARP SPINE

A knife with a sharp spine means that you don't have to carry an extra striker to use with a ferrocerium rod. In addition, the spine can be used like a cabinet scraper when processing fine tinder materials from soft woods or fatwood pine. It also allows for fast removal of outer barks. Using the knife spine for these operations will save the sharp blade for when you need it.

1
2
3
4
5
6
7
8
9

CARBON STEEL

Carbon steel, when heat-treated correctly, allows you to use your knife as a steel for flint-and-steel fire starting. More importantly, it is easier to resharpen carbon steel or maintain its sharp edge than it is for stainless or other complex types of super steels.

4" TO 5" BLADE

When considering a belt knife from a survival standpoint, remember that one of its main functions must be processing wood for anything from shelter building to creating fire lay materials. You won't need pieces more than 4" in diameter for the short term if you are using green wood for structures and dry wood for fire starting.

SIMPLE GRIND

Simple **knife grinds** have a single bevel, like a V grind or saber to zero grinds. This allows for ease of sharpening without multiple grinds. A simple convex grind can be maintained with a belt strap as well, but a simple knife grind will make the job easier for people.

Glossary

A-frame shelter
A shelter with two walls meeting at the top, which can deflect wind or rain from two sides.

aiming off
In navigation, to take a bearing to the left or right of the intended destination by a few degrees so that when you get to that bearing, you know whether to turn right or left to reach your destination.

azimuth
A bearing, or the direction in which you are traveling; the angle of deviation of a bearing from a standard direction, such as north or south.

backstop
In navigation, a point beyond which you shouldn't go. Generally, a linear feature that runs perpendicular to the route to your destination.

bank line
Tarred nylon used for fishing and net making. It is a good survival cord, as it is rot- and UV-resistant.

baseline
The opposite of backstops, baselines run perpendicular to your point of departure and provide a means of getting back to where you started from.

batoning
A means of splitting wood by using a stick (or "baton") to strike your knife and drive it through a piece of wood such as a log.

bearing
In navigation, direction.

bezel ring
A movable ring on a compass indicating directions marked in degrees. It is used in orienting.

binding
Made of cordage, bindings are used to keep objects from coming apart or separating. For example, a binding on the end of a rope keeps the strands from fraying.

bird's nest
Used in fire starting, this is a bundle of tinder shaped roughly like a bird's nest. It should be a combination of fine, medium, and coarse highly combustible materials.

bivy bag
A plastic bag that covers the camper's head and sleeping bag to protect against the elements or damp ground. Derived from the word "bivouac."

bow drill
A fire-making method that uses a bow to move a stick rapidly, generating friction and heat to ignite tinder.

browse bag
A lightweight bag sewn up one side and across one end. It can be filled with material to make a mattress.

canvas
Material used mainly for tarps and tarp tents. It is waterproof, usually fireproof, and mildew-resistant.

deadfall
Wood that has naturally fallen—dead branches, trees blown over, and so on.

declination
Part of a map legend; gives the amount of degree offset left or right between magnetic north and map north.

decoction
A drink made from material such as roots or bark, which is boiled before drinking.

diamond layout
This shelter is anchored by three corners to the ground, while the fourth corner is fastened to a tree or some other structure, creating a diamond shape.

draw
The reduction in elevation from a saddle with high ground on both sides.

fatwood
The resinous area of a pine tree in which sap collects naturally. Excellent as fire-starting material.

feather sticks
Sticks that are cut to create bunches of shavings on one end. This creates additional surface area, making feather sticks useful for starting fires.

fell

To cut wood, especially trees. Felling a tree is not a decision to be taken lightly.

ferrocerium rod

A rod made from pyrophoric materials used to start fires by striking it against a hard surface, which produces sparks.

fire lay

Wood laid in a particular pattern to start a fire.

flying a tarp

A method of setting up a tarp in which none of it touches the ground.

hammock

A bed you can swing between two supports off the ground. It protects you from crawling creatures and prevents the loss of body heat through conduction.

handrails

Linear objects within the terrain that you can use as a guide line to follow when they lead in the intended direction of travel.

kindling

Material that can be easily ignited to start a fire.

knife grind

The shape of the cross section of a knife blade. Different grinds require you to hold your whetstone at different angles when sharpening the blade.

lashing

Knots used to fasten several objects together. These are essential in constructing sturdy shelters in the wild.

lateral drift

The tendency, when walking long distances, to gradually move left or right.

lean-to

A shelter made from a single wall propped up at an angle and covered with leaves, branches, and other debris to form a secure roof.

magnifying glass

A lens used for close examination of anything, as well as a reliable firestarter in the wilderness.

notching

Carving notches in a branch or pole, either for construction or to create hangers and handles.

pace beads

Strands of beads used to keep track of distance while walking. Once you determine your pace, you drop a bead on the strand after walking a given number of paces.

parachute cord

A cord with a woven outer covering (the mantle) that protects the inner strands that give the cord its strength.

PAUL method

Stands for Positive Azimuth Uniform Layout. This method allows you to scout an unfamiliar area and figure a straight line bearing back to camp without backtracking by reverse azimuths the entire way.

pitching a tarp

To stake any part of a tarp at ground level.

poultice

Heated or cooled plant material applied to the body like a bandage or as a remedy for illness.

resin

The sap of a pine tree. It can be used as a firestarter, a bandage for a wound, and for various medicinal purposes.

ridgeline

On maps, a series of hilltops, offering an observation point and high-ground travel. Also, a rope or cord that is tied between two points lengthwise that forms the top of a shelter.

Roycroft or Roycraft frame

A frame for carrying your pack. It consists of three sticks lashed together to form a triangle.

saddle

A lower-lying area between two hilltops that forms a drainage point for the hilltops as well as protection from wind and rain.

shear cut

A cut made to shear off wood from a larger piece.

sheath

A case or covering for a bladed tool.

sleeping bag

Any of a number of padded bags made for sleeping. They can be insulated with feathers, down, artificial insulation, or air space, among other things.

tannin
An astringent derived from the oak tree. It can be used to make poultices, infusions, and dyes.

tarp
Short for "tarpaulin"; a canvas or oilskin covering used to erect shelters and for other purposes in the wild.

tinder, tinder bundles
Highly combustible material that can readily take a spark or easily catch fire when a smoldering ember is added.

toggle
A wood stick or dowel connected to a line by a knot. This can be used as an attachment point that is easily moved or removed, and can be load bearing if needed.

tubular webbing
Webbing used primarily for climbing. It weighs less than rope, takes up less space, and generally has higher tensile strength.

Venturi effect
The tendency of air entering a narrowing tube to flow faster. This can have a significant effect on a fire.

widowmakers

Standing dead trees that may fall or break if subjected to wind. These could cause serious safety issues.

Index

About the Author

Dave Canterbury is the co-owner and supervising instructor at The Pathfinder School, which *USA TODAY* named as one of the Top 12 Survival Schools in the United States. He has been published in *Self Reliance Illustrated*, *The New Pioneer*, *American Frontiersman*, and *Trapper's World*. Dave is the *New York Times* bestselling author of *Bushcraft 101*; *Advanced Bushcraft*; and *The Bushcraft Field Guide to Trapping, Gathering, & Cooking in the Wild*.

FIELD NOTES

FIELD NOTES

FIELD NOTES

FIELD NOTES

FIELD NOTES

FIELD NOTES

FIELD NOTES

FIELD NOTES

FIELD NOTES

FIELD NOTES

FIELD NOTES

FIELD NOTES

FIELD NOTES

FIELD NOTES

FIELD NOTES

FIELD NOTES

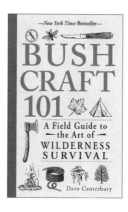